FORGIVE

AND

GET YOUR LIFE BACK

DENNIS R. MAYNARD, D.MIN.

FORGIVE AND GET YOUR LIFE BACK

COPYRIGHT © 2001 BY DENNIS R. MAYNARD, D.MIN

ISBN: 188598503-7

DIONYSUS PUBLICATIONS
49 VIA DEL ROSSI
RANCHO MIRAGE, CA 92270
760-324-8589
Episkopols@aol.com
www.Episkopols.com

CREATIVE SERVICES AND PRINTING THROUGH:
CSN BOOKS PUBLISHING
1975 JANICH RANCH COURT
EL CAJON, CA 92019-1150
TOLL FREE: 1-866-484-6184
www.CSNbooks.com

PRINTED IN THE UNITED STATES OF AMERICA

Forgive and Forget! We have all heard it. We may have even uttered those words ourselves. But how? When our hearts have been torn out of our chests and our entire bodies numbed by the pain, just how does one go about forgiving and forgetting? Rare is the person who does not want their nightmare of suffering to come to an end. This book is written from a pastoral perspective. The Reverend Doctor Dennis Maynard, an Episcopal Priest, has spent thirty-four years leading thousands of people through the forgiveness process. Reading the following pages is like sitting with him in his study and having a quiet pastoral chat. This book is filled with practical suggestions and moving illustrations. The words on these pages will not only guide the reader through the process of forgiving, but inspire them with the hope that they too, can forgive and get their life back.

DEDICATION

You can see them in airports, restaurants, at work, and in the Houses of Worship of every religion. Their eyes are often hollow and lifeless. Humor is a stranger to their homes. Tears are but a grimace away. Sleep eludes them. They are unable to eat or even sit still for the briefest period of time.

Some wear smiles without light. Their laughter is without joy. Often they robotically live out their days by anesthetizing their pain with busyness, work, food, prescription drugs, alcohol, sex or any addiction designed to fill the hole that is in their heart.

Others look sullen. Their faces have been set in stone. Their jaws are locked. Flashes of anger stand ready to be ignited. They look at the world through the bifocals of self-pity and contempt. They too have been hurt.

Recently or in the distant past, each of these souls has been wounded by an act of betrayal, accident, or catastrophe. Each lives with a heartache that will not go away. Their lives have been frozen in a moment in time when they discovered their reality was but an illusion.

This book is dedicated to them. I want to help them get their lives back. To do so requires that they must do the unthinkable. They must forgive the very one who inflicted the pain upon them. Until they forgive them, their lives are irrevocably chained to those who hurt them. Their very lives have been frozen in a traumatic moment in time. They are tortured prisoners of the past.

This book is dedicated to the healing of the wounded soul.

TABLE OF CONTENTS

"The Lord shall renew your strength; you shall mount up with wings as eagles; you shall run, and not be weary; and you shall walk, and not faint." (Isaiah 40:31)

INTRODUCTION

All my life I have been told to "forgive and forget." I have uttered these words to others and I have repeated them to myself. "Let go of it! Move on! Forget it!" **But how? How do you go about forgiving and forgetting? It is not as easy as it sounds!** Forgiveness becomes especially difficult in light of the various ways one human being can bring pain upon another. The possibilities are endless. Some of the most destructive stories of our inhumanity to one another come out of war, persecution, and the various blood baths that mar human history. Whether we call them racial, religious, or ethnic cleansing, the stories themselves wreak with tragedy. One wonders how those subjected to such torment can ever forgive the nightmare that was inflicted on them and their loved ones. Archbishop Desmond Tutu reminds us "without forgiveness there is no future."

I can still recall seeing the December 1998 issue of *Life* magazine. There was a full picture of a group of protestors with twisted, bitter, anger-filled faces, only they were not standing outside the White House or in front of a military establishment. They were holding a sign in big letters that read, "FREEDOM OF CHOICE IS THE RIGHT TO HATE!" This sign and those who supported this sentiment were standing outside the funeral of Matthew Shepherd. This young twenty-one year old gay student had been beaten to death and hanged cross-like on a fence in Laramie, Wyoming. His family and friends had to pass by this hate-filled group of people in order to bury their child that had been subjected to such brutality. How can they or any of us ever learn to forgive those who have disrupted our lives or the life of someone we love? How can we ever let go of the hurt and pain and not give in to our instinct for revenge? How can we bring our respective nightmares to an end?

Whether we have been the target of a hate crime or experienced the brutality of violence our ultimate healing is dependent on our ability to forgive. If someone we trusted has betrayed our love and friendship that pain too has the ability to paralyze us. It can turn us into bitter, revenge-filled people. It can harden our hearts and bury us in a grave marked by a hurtful moment in time. How will we ever be able to let go of the pain? How will we ever learn to trust again?

The articles in popular magazines remind us that when we forgive others we will feel better. We will improve our mental, emotional, and physical health. The motivation to forgive is there, but the hurt remains. And just when we think that we have forgiven and put the pain behind us it can come back to haunt us months, even years later.

FORGIVENESS IS A PROCESS

Forgiveness is a process. True forgiveness will cost us something! Just as the hurt that shattered our faith and trust in another came at considerable expense to us emotionally and physically, forgiving will also come with a price. The trauma of betrayal will not be erased simply by uttering words of forgiveness. The days or weeks of our life that we have spent numbed by the sting of betrayal will not be easily forgotten. We will be slammed with disbelief the rest of our lives. The paralyzing humiliation will be remembered again and again. The pain that has been inflicted on us and gripped our hearts like a vise has left them bruised, tender, and hollow. Our souls are wounded. Our spirits are broken. The earth literally ceases to spin for us as we come to grips with the unimaginable. The betrayal has cost us and will cost us. Forgiving those who have hurt us will also come at a price. The pain or the trauma of betrayal may have been thrown into our lives in a matter of seconds. Forgiveness will take time. Just as the body takes time to heal from a piercing wound, so does the soul. Please be patient with yourself.

Several books on forgiveness are already available. I have read many of them. Each book can be helpful at some level. No one book can do the work of forgiveness for us. Still, I dare to make my contribution to the healing process in this book. I do so because I know that forgiveness is easier to talk about than to do. I know that it is easier to encourage others to forgive than it is to do so oneself. Above all else, I make this offering because I believe it critical that those who minister to the wounded soul must always be mindful of the fact that forgiveness is a spiritual work.

THIS BOOK IS A SELF-HELP GUIDE
TO FORGIVING

The unique offering of this book is that it is intended to be a self-help guide to assist you through the forgiveness process. When portions of this book were first published in 1994 under the title of *Forgiven, Healed, and Restored* I found that some of those who showed the greatest interest and support were members of the medical community. In particular, I was especially encouraged by the members of the psychiatric and therapeutic community. I received special encouragement from Dr. Bill Moore M.D., a practicing psychiatrist in Houston, Texas and a member of St. Martin's Episcopal Church. Three thousand copies of that book were purchased, many of them by mental health practitioners and clergy to give to their patients or for use in study and support groups. Perhaps there is no other arena where the spiritual and the psychological join hands so completely as in the process of forgiving and being forgiven.

It is my hope that this book will not only directly assist those who choose to read it, but that it will be a resource to members of the helping professions to use with those in their care who have been wounded. For this reason I have included some Reflection/Action Questions at the end of each chapter. These questions are intended to assist a wounded person through the forgiveness process. The questions can be used for individual reflection or for reflection and action planning in a small group devoted to healing.

FORGIVENESS IS A SPIRITUAL WORK

Scientist, theologian Teilhard de Chardin made the observation that "we are not human beings in search of a spiritual experience, but we are spiritual beings having a human experience." If during our human experience our spirit has been wounded, the human tools that find their origin in self-effort will be inadequate for the task of spiritual healing. Even religion in its best-dressed robes of piety and dogma may leave the spiritual work of forgiveness incomplete. There is a popular expression; "religion is for people who fear they might go to hell. Spirituality is for people who have already been there." Those who have had their reality shattered understand the torments of a living hell. Forgiveness is a spiritual work.

ON THE OTHER SIDE OF THE PAIN YOU MAY NOW BE FEELING THERE IS LAUGHTER AND JOY.

My ultimate objective is to lead you through to the other side of your hurt and anguish. I will point the way to a brighter day. I will hold before you a time when wholeness will be restored to your life. On the other side of the pain you may now be feeling there is laughter and joy. When we are deep into our suffering, it is difficult for us to believe that we will ever be able to trust again. It is difficult to believe that we will ever be able to love again. During times of emotional famine laughter is a stranger to our house. The warmth has escaped through the shattered windows. On those occasions, it is imperative that we hold onto the hope that joy will once again be a possibility for us. Holding out this possibility can sound dismissive of our current hurt. But just as the runner always looks to the finish line, so too, they still have to run every step of the race. They cannot escape the aches in their sides, the blurry vision, muscles straining, and bones hurting, or the haunting question that they just might not be able to finish the course. In the same way, there are no easy, pain-free shortcuts to forgiveness.

Forgiving and Reconciling are not the Same Thing

On these pages I will also strive to make some critical distinctions between forgiveness, reconciliation, and restoration. Forgiveness brings healing. It is the key that unlocks the doors to the torturous chamber we are currently calling home. However, we may or may not reconcile with the person we have forgiven. Restoring them to their former place in our lives is yet another decision. This book will define each separately so that we can make our decisions about each one individually. This may be one of the most unique offerings of this particular book. It is imperative that we understand that we can find healing for ourselves by forgiving those who have hurt us without reconciling with them. Obviously, reconciliation is the ideal. Restoration is the ultimate objective. There are those occasions, those circumstances, and particular people when neither reconciliation nor restoration is desirable or even possible. In those cases, forgiveness still remains the only pathway for setting ourselves free and getting our lives back.

I am grateful to Dr. Barbara Parry, M.D., Professor of Psychiatric Medicine at the University of California San Diego School of Medicine and to Dr. Viola Frymann, D.O. Both Dr. Frymann and Dr. Parry have reviewed this manuscript and made many positive suggestions. Dr. Parry speaks forcefully for blending the spiritual and the psychological. Dr. Frymann, a former associate of evangelist Katherine Kuhlman, is well-known among practitioners of Osteopathic Medicine around the world for her work with children which brings the spiritual and the medical together in the healing process.

If you are hurting right now, may God use the words and insights in this book to return laughter to your house.

Dennis Maynard
Spring, 2003

Step One

"Choose to Forgive"

The Walking Wounded live life daily anchored to some past hurt or betrayal. The memory of the pain can be overwhelming. The desire for revenge can fill us with bitterness, anxiety, the fear of being hurt again. In order to get our life back we have to do the unthinkable. We have to make the conscious decision to forgive the very ones who have injured us.

You look hurt! Try as we may, we humans are not able to hide our pain. We may paste a plastic smile on our face, but it does not reach our eyes. It does not come from our soul. We can defensively try to control every detail of our life, but try as we may we will not be able to control the pain that brews inside us. We will not be able to prevent additional hurts coming our direction. The short temper, the wrinkled brow, the arch in our back all give us away. We have been hurt. We look hurt.

Through some act of betrayal our world has been turned upside down. Perhaps the person that has brought all this pain into our life was someone we knew, loved, and trusted. Or, we may have been victimized by a stranger. The pain is the same.

1

We are paralyzed with disbelief. Physically, our body is in turmoil. We no longer feel safe. We are not in control of our universe.

In most cases of betrayal, sleep will elude us. We will not want to eat. We will literally walk around in a daze. The word "anxiety" takes on new meaning as we try to answer all the questions for ourselves.

"Why did this happen?

What did I do to deserve this?

Why me?

What am I going to do next?

How am I going to get through this?"

When we have been hurt, the circumstances surrounding the betrayal are often beyond our control. There would have been little, if anything, we could have done to change the situation. Those bent on hurting us will, in spite of our best efforts, find a way to accomplish their goal. We are not victims by our choice. However, we do have a choice. We get to choose the way we respond to the hurts inflicted on us by others in this life.

DON'T BE HELD HOSTAGE

As much as we might will ourselves to stop hurting we cannot magically make the pain go away. It would take a monumental effort on our part not to blame the person responsible for bringing all this suffering into our lives. We feel like a victim precisely because we are one. Our lamb's coat appears pure white to us simply because it is dripping with emotional blood – our own. Our anger is justified. We believe we are entitled to our resentments.

When we have been hurt our human tendency is to wallow in our pain. We want to blame the person that hurt us. We reason that we are more pure than they are. We are tempted to present ourselves as the one without sin. We are beyond reproach. We would never yield to such a temptation. Our bitterness is justified. We believe that we are entitled to our resentments. We reason, "Why should we forgive them? If we forgive them, it will only make them feel better. Why should we do that?" In the aftermath of the pain we erroneously reason that by not forgiving those who have hurt us, we can make them suffer. If we withhold our forgiveness they will come crawling back to us on their knees. By nurturing our hurt and anger we can make them see just how much they hurt us and their guilt will be increased.

Just as physical pain can twist our thinking, so too, can emotional pain. Some wounded animals withdraw into a cloak of self-protection. People can be no different. We can withdraw into a cloak of self-protection, assume the role of victim. We can attempt to present our scars as evidence of our own virtue. "After all that I have done for them," can become our mantra. We can attempt to use our hurt to gain sympathy from others. We can wear our wounds as battle scars. We want them to be painful reminders to the one who inflicted them on us. Perhaps if we play the pitiful game well enough we will actually develop our own stigmata. We can feed off the sympathy and pity of those around us.

If we choose to nurture our pain, then we have also chosen to live our lives as a person with no future. We choose to live in the past. The past in fact becomes our burial garment. We simply are waiting on our interment.

Recently, I was at a wedding rehearsal dinner. Seated next to me was a woman in her fifties who had recently divorced her husband of twenty-eight years. Seated directly in front of us at the adjacent table and in our direct line of vision were the ex-husband and his new wife who was at least twenty years his junior.

Clearly, the first wife seated next to me had been hurt. It was common knowledge in the community that her husband had been having the affair that led to his current marriage for some time. Regardless of the circumstances of the marriage or the character of the first wife, the pain of betrayal that she was enduring could not be justified in any arena of human relationships. She had been wounded. Her heart was still tender. Her hurt was real.

Throughout the evening the ex-wife sitting next to me chose to express her pain by shooting her "ex and his new squeeze" hate-filled looks. The poison oozed out of her system as she rehearsed for me with minute detail his betrayal. Her words were vindictive and cutting. For nearly two and one half-hours her former husband and his new "twinkie" consumed her.

As we stood to leave the banquet she stated, "Now you can understand why I am so happy to be rid of him." I countered, "But you are not rid of him. You are more married to him right now than you have ever been. In fact, you are his prisoner. He has total control over you. Until you forgive him you have completely bound yourself to him and to his new wife. You are their captive. The only way you will ever be rid of him is to forgive him. It is the only way you can cut the chains of anger and hatred that have locked you together with them. Once you do that you will get your life back. You will be free to live without him. His every action will stop consuming you. It is the only way you will truly be rid of him."

I will never forget the words she shot back at me; "I'll never give him the satisfaction. Forgive him? I'll see him burn in hell first even if I have to go down there with him to stoke the fire."

As she spun to walk away, I grabbed her arm. "It is not about his satisfaction. It is about your satisfaction. It is about

4

getting your life back." She shook her arm free of my hand and shared with me one of the looks that she had so freely given her ex-husband all evening.

Martyrs make lousy party guests. If we choose the role of victim and use our wounds to gain sympathy, we hurt ourselves more than we hurt the offender. If we choose to harden our hearts and act out our hurts in an effort to hurt the other or gain some form of revenge, we hurt ourselves more than we hurt the offender. What we need to come to understand is that the unforgiving heart is self-destructive. In fact, we choose to live our lives being held hostage by those who have hurt us.

> IF WE NURTURE OUR HURT, OUR ENTIRE SPIRITUAL SYSTEM IS POISONED. WE BECOME INFECTIOUS. WE MAY CONTAMINATE EVERYONE AROUND US.

REVENGE IS CONTAGIOUS

Not only do we choose to be held hostage, but if we nurture our hurt, our entire spiritual system is poisoned. We become infectious. We run the risk of contaminating everyone around us. We may even end up destroying the lives of the very people we profess to love. Let me share with you parts of a letter that was written to me several years ago. I have amended the names, characters, details and pertinent places to protect the identity of the writer. It is one of the most powerful testaments for the need to forgive that I have ever received. From this letter it is unclear as to whether or not the wife was actually betrayed by her husband or even the true nature of the betrayal if there was one. Obviously she was hurt in some way and she held her husband responsible for her pain. The focus of the letter centers not around the circumstances of the marital discord, but on the destructive nature of anger and resentment. Because the wife described in this scenario was unwilling to forgive and chose rather to nurture her pain and anger for a lifetime, not only did she destroy her own life, but came close to destroying the lives of her children as well.

This letter is offered as an example of the destructive consequences of choosing revenge over forgiveness. It challenges us to ask ourselves if we want to use our own hurt to destroy the lives of others.

My parents divorced when I was 12. My father moved to a house at the end of our block, where the four of us children lived with my mother, who had custody of us. My father had visitation rights, and we visited him on Sundays. He wanted to be close to us, so he bought the house at the end of our street. Neither he nor my mother ever remarried, and they remained living one block apart for thirty years, not speaking to each other, until he died.

I have only a few good memories of childhood. From as far back as I can remember, there was tension between my father and mother, and I don't remember them ever talking to each other, touching each other, holding hands, hugging or having the kind of relationship that I now have with my husband. When I was about four or five years old, the fighting and arguing began, mostly about money and about the long hours my father worked. When I was ten or eleven, my mother filed for divorce. After a bitter court battle, in which we children were involved at one point, the divorce became final. I was thirteen years old, and my life was shattered.

But, as traumatic and tragic as the divorce was, it was not the divorce itself that so deeply scarred all of

6

us. *It was the fact that there was no respect, no compassion, no mutual understanding and, above all, no forgiveness between my mother and father. My mother adopted an "us against him" mentality, insisting that my father was "the evil one" and she "the good one" in the marriage. I realize now that it was insecurity that caused this. My mother needed to feel that we children loved her more than we loved our father. After years of listening to my mother and her lady friends disparage my father in front of us children; after years of my mother's programming me to believe my father hated me; after years of seeing him through the negative, bitter, resentful eyes of my mother, I became a very lost and confused person. Although deep inside I still loved my father, I buried those feelings of love and practiced the hatred I had learned. I became very disrespectful of him, which I believe was the beginning of all misfortune in my life.*

I did not have the courage to stand up to my mother as a child, for obvious reasons, and even if I had, I was so influenced by everything she said that I was unable to sort out the truth from her perceived reality. This pattern continued throughout my adolescence and young adulthood, so that when I became engaged to be married to my first husband, an alcoholic, at the age of 20, I listened to my mother's advice and did not allow my father to walk me down the aisle and give me away at my wedding. I can still remember her telling me how he was never a father to me and that he could be invited to the wedding as a guest, but should not be acknowledged as my father. Only her name appeared on the wedding invitation. Looking back on this, I cannot believe how much hurt my father endured, yet he continued to love us. My marriage – which never should have taken place, I now realize—dissolved in less than a year.

My father was not a saint, by any stretch of the imagination. He was an ordinary man, with good and bad qualities, some that made him extremely difficult to live with. A musician by calling, he followed his dream and pursued a career. He formed his own orchestra and played in clubs all over the Northwest. He met and fell in love with my mother during this time. According to all my dad's family members, theirs was a beautiful love affair. I did not understand as a child how difficult it must have been for my father to have to divide his life between his love of music and his love for my mother and desire to have a family. He made many sacrifices, taking a job with an aircraft assembly plant to buy a house and pay the bills, while teaching music on weeknights and performing with his orchestra on the weekends. This, I now know, was at the root of my parent's disagreements.

My mother's criticism of him and her increasingly non-supportive attitude led to her gossiping about him with family members and her lady friends, always pulling us children into the middle of it. We learned to laugh at my father and make him the butt of jokes. We learned to criticize his Italian heritage. We learned not only to marginalize him, but also to "erase" him from our lives. We learned to focus all our negativity and to project our own anxieties and resentments about life onto him. He became the reason for everything that went wrong in our lives. When the four of us children were summoned to court to talk to the divorce court judge, I remember, as does my younger brother, my mother coaching us to say we did not want to visit our father (although visitation was ultimately granted). He became as victimized as my mother perceived herself to be. It was classic scapegoat theory.

Over the years, I forgot all the good things my father did. I forgot that he would bundle the four of us up in the wintertime after visiting family on Sundays (Sunday was always church and family day) and carry us, one by one, from the house to the car through the cold and snow. I forgot that he taught me how to save money and watch the interest grow. I forgot that he would bring the four of us little presents from the store every payday. I forgot that he was a good, Christian man whose guidelines were the Ten Commandments. I forgot that he engraved Biblical passages onto little sterling silver pendants, shaped and polished them, and made them into jewelry for my sister and me. I forgot he gave me my first prayer book when I was confirmed in the Episcopal Church. I forgot that he would take us on Sundays for ice cream cones after church, to the library, to the museum, and to concerts in the park, and that he instilled in each of us a love for culture and the arts. I forgot so much.

Throughout it all, the negative and disparaging remarks about my father never ceased. Her bitterness, resentment, and negativity turned to rage over the years, resulting in a manipulated and devised image of my father as something inhuman. She referred to him as sadistic. She told me he hated me because I looked like her. She said he never came to the hospital when she gave birth to us children because he hated us. Over the years, the thoughts grew more and more negative and the remarks more vicious to the extent that he was referred to, at various times throughout our lives, as a monster, a homosexual, and a wife beater. None of these things were true. Then, a few years ago, right after my *husband and I married, my sister came out with the allegation that, through the help of her counselor, she had recovered some memories from childhood and learned that over the course of eight years, my father had sexually molested her. She said that it was because of this that she was unable to have an intimate relationship with a man and was becoming a lesbian. My sister and I slept in the same bed until I was eighteen years old. I knew, as did my eldest sister and younger brother, that the allegation was untrue.*

My father is now gone. Early last year, he was diagnosed with prostate cancer at age 78. I had developed a relationship with him only a few years prior. I had caused a huge stir in my family when I invited him to my college graduation. I was thirty-six years old, and for the first time in my life, I broke the family rules and included my father in a family event. Looking back on it, and on all the criticism I received for it from my mother and sister, I realize that this was, and continues to be, my cross in life. My mother and sister boycotted my graduation. They accused me of being controlling and malicious in trying to bring my dad into the family.

My father died in our home four years ago. He died exactly three months after being diagnosed with cancer. My youngest brother finally came around toward the very end. On his deathbed, my father gave my youngest brother the pocket watch that had belonged to his father. When my sister came, she had not spoken to him in over five years. My father sobbed uncontrollably when he saw her. She did not hug him or cry. When he said his final good-byes to each of us, he hugged us one by one. He saved my sister for last. Once again, as he said her name, he held out his arms to her, he sobbed and held her tight.

My mother came to our house to visit with my father several times during his last weeks. She had not set foot in our house nor spoken to my husband in over six years, and she had not spoken to my father in over thirty years. She showed no emotion. She said she had apologized to my father, but that the apology he had given in return was not sufficient for her.

He's gone from us now, and we four children have inherited equally everything he possessed and worked for all his life. He provided very well for all of us. He had a beautiful funeral. Hundreds of people came to the funeral home, including classmates going back to his elementary school days, as well as his high school prom date. His musician friends performed for him. Everyone I talked to said the same things about my dad: He was the best friend one could hope to have, and a gentleman always.

A few months ago, while in our basement continuing to sort through the boxes in my dad's personal belongings, I came across a letter. It was a letter that my youngest brother had written to him six years ago, following my niece's wedding at which my brother would not speak to my father, and just a couple of years before he was diagnosed with cancer. The letter said that my brother did not recognize him as his father, and that nowhere in the Bible does it say that a son has to love a father who has raped his daughter. My father had written in the margins of the letter, in a feeble hand, denying the charge. He wrote that he loved all of us and had supported us as best he could. Through everything my father saved, I saw a helpless man who knew that he would never be able to convince his children of his love for us, and one who had spent a lifetime documenting that he was a good person.

I found court papers stemming from the divorce, and psychiatric evaluations performed on my father at that time that indicated that he was not a harmful or violent man but was acting on the feeling that his authority in the family had been subverted. The reports stated that he felt anxious and helpless and behaved in a way in which any man in his situation would typically behave. I also found every cancelled check he ever wrote, many written to my sister during her college years, although she had maintained that he never gave her anything to help her. I found hundreds of photographs that my dad had taken of us children, many of which I had never before seen, like a documentary in black and white of the years of Sundays that we had spent together. I found all the cards from his and my mother's wedding and bridal shower, which had been tucked away in a box in the back of his bedroom closet. And I found programs from every event that my siblings and I ever performed in, such as school concerts. On each one, he had circled our names in ink or pencil. I didn't even remember my father being there.

What hurts most are the cards I found that he attempted to send us children following the separation, but were marked "Return to Sender" in my mother's handwriting. They were still unopened. They were birthday and Christmas cards dating back to the '60s. What hurts as much are the letters I found that he wrote, but never sent. One was a letter to my mother's parents, written by an admittedly desperate man, during the time preceding the divorce. In it, he said that he had never asked my mother's parents for anything, but that he was begging them now for help. He begged them to talk to their daughter. He said he would give her anything she wanted if she would rescind the divorce action, as he loved her, and divorce was against his religious beliefs. He said that we children had been exposed to so much hatred that we were sure to have difficulty in adulthood and may be inclined to not marry, after all that we had witnessed. He was right.

What I can't get over is the hurt and pain he endured. I hurt when I think about all the weddings, anniversary parties, and family celebrations my dad performed at throughout his life, yet he never had the honor of performing at one of his own children's events. How many times had he performed the father-daughter dance for the bride and her dad, and watched them dance together, and how did he endure what I had done to him at my first wedding? How many silver and golden anniversary parties did he perform at, only to long for just one day with my mother? How many of our school concerts did he attend, and afterwards watch from the sidelines as we left with my mother, oblivious to his presence, longing to be part of our lives again? How many days, nights, years, decades did he sit in his living room or on his front porch at the end of our street, waiting, hoping that one of his children would voluntarily walk down to his house to visit him, or that the phone would ring and he would hear one of our voices? We never called. We never came.

All of this is to say that unwillingness to forgive is lethal, not only to the one needing forgiveness, but also to the one whose forgiveness is not forthcoming. My family is proof. The implications span generations. When there is a lack of forgiveness, everyone, especially the children suffer.

FORGIVING WILL SET US FREE!

I remember reading about a research project that was conducted at Hope College in Holland, Michigan. They asked volunteers to think about someone who had hurt them. As they dwelt on their resentments, the subjects showed greater physiological distress, including more rapid heartbeat and an increase in their blood pressure. Even their facial expressions became distorted. After they were told to stop thinking about the person and the events, the signs of physiological distress did not abate, but continued.

These subjects were then asked to imagine what it would feel like to forgive the person that had hurt them. They reported a more peaceful feeling. They reported that they were happier and more in control. The researchers reported that the subject's physiological systems relaxed.

Nurturing anger, resentment, and hurt is self-destructive. Our serenity and peace are found not in focusing on our hurts, but in developing a forgiving heart. Anger and resentment bring harm to us. We become diseased. The original understanding of this word "disease" has nothing to do with viruses and bacteria. It is "dis-ease" in our souls. Our harmony has been destroyed. Resentment destroys our harmony. Grace and forgiveness bring healing and wholeness. Our souls, our very beings are put in a state of ease.

How we respond to the hurts in our life is our decision. As I said earlier, we do not choose to be victims, but we do get to choose how we are going to manage the hurt and pain. It is a choice we make. We can choose to send those who hurt us messages of anger and revenge. Or we can choose to send them love, forgiveness, and grace. If we choose not to forgive those who have hurt us, we simply must understand that we also choose to become prisoners of our own misery. We make the decision to have our futures buried in a grave marked by a past hurt.

Freedom is a Choice

If I have learned only one thing in thirty-four years of pastoral ministry with hundreds people coast to coast in this country, it is that the inability to forgive those who have hurt us is self-destructive. The primary source of unhappiness for an awfully lot of people is their inability to forgive. The suffering in our lives is determined by the way we choose to respond to the hurtful blows we have received.

We can choose to move through our pain. We can choose to learn from it. We can choose to use the desert times in our lives as times to grow and develop. We can choose to have the pain help us discover our own inner strength. It can be a time for growing in grace. When we do, we are set free to live, laugh, and love again. The choice is always ours. Do we send hatred for hatred? Or, do we issue forgiveness in the face of our own hurt and pain? When we withhold forgiveness, we begin a path of self-destruction. When we respond with forgiveness, we bring healing. We set ourselves free.

God, our Higher Power, makes forgiveness possible. It is the Almighty's way of restoring healing and hope in our lives. It is God's way of giving our lives back to us after we have been traumatized. We do not have to do it all alone. God can and will do it through us if we choose. It is the only way that the "dis-ease" in our souls can be healed and harmony restored. Forgiveness is a gift. Forgiveness is a gift that we can give to others. It is one of the greatest gifts that we can give ourselves. Forgiveness is a process. It can only be accomplished one step at a time. The first step is to make the decision to **forgive and get your life back**.

QUESTIONS FOR REFLECTION AND/OR ACTION

1. Can you think of ways you have tried to deny the reality of your hurt? Do you know people who live a life denying their pain? Do you want to be one of them?

2. Do you know people who play the martyr? Do you enjoy being around them? If you choose to be a martyr how would you do it? Will people want to be around you?

3. How would you get revenge on the person that has hurt you? What makes you think it will make you feel better? Do you know bitter people hardened by their pain? Do you really want to be one of them?

4. Would you like to stop hurting? Do you really want to "turn off the video" and cease living in the past? Imagine what it would be like to feel good again?

STEP TWO

"DON'T CRY ALONE"

Some of us are afraid to tell anyone about our hurt. We fear the embarrassment of having others know that our trust was betrayed. Some blame themselves for having been so vulnerable... so stupid. Some of us can't stop talking about our hurt and just how awful those who betrayed us really are. Some of us talk and talk and talk. We will talk to anyone who will listen. We simply can't stop ourselves from complaining about the source of our pain. Most people we know have already grown tired of listening.

The story is told of the little girl who was late walking home from school. Her parents were worried. When she finally arrived home they asked, "Where have you been?"

"I was walking home with Susan," the little girl explained. "She dropped her doll on the sidewalk and it broke into pieces."

"Oh," her parents inquired. "Did you stay to help her pick up the pieces?"

"No," their daughter exclaimed. "I stayed to help her cry."

The great danger for any of us that have been hurt is to try to deny or minimize the pain. There is a tendency to be dismissive of the trauma our hearts have suffered. Folks ask, "Aren't you upset? Doesn't it hurt?" We too easily shrug our shoulders, "Oh, I'm alright. I'll get through this. Don't worry about me."

The real truth is that often we don't want to have to deal with the depth of our hurt. This is especially true if we judge the act that has brought pain into our lives as embarrassing or humiliating. We fear that the embarrassment of having others know that our trust has been violated would be more painful than the act itself. We worry about what others will think of us. We may choose to suffer in silence. We choose to keep their violation secret. We become co-conspirators with the very people that have hurt us. We become willing accomplices in their act of betrayal. We not only must suffer the repercussions of their deeds, but we agree to cover up for them.

It is imperative that we understand that we do not keep secrets. Our secrets keep us! We have to understand that if we fail to deal with the hurt today it will show up in our tomorrows. We have to realize that the betrayal of those who hurt us is not information about us. Their words and deeds are information about them. Denying our hurt, denying the reality of their actions will not make the hurt go away. Denial is a choice, but it is not a choice that will lead to our healing and wholeness.

In order to negate the pain, we need to talk about it. We need to share our hurt with another human being. Verbalizing our hurt is an integral part of the healing process.

We need to hear ourselves talk about the attack on our hearts, our souls, and our very egos. We need a trusted friend, counselor, priest, rabbi, or support group. Depending on the depth of the betrayal, we may need a combination of several support systems.

Talking Keeps Us from Becoming Paralyzed in Denial

One of the primary benefits of talking with another person about our pain is that it prevents us from becoming paralyzed in denial. I have often witnessed people first comprehending the scope of the betrayal and the depth of their pain by hearing themselves verbalize it for the first time.

Likewise, verbalizing the circumstances of our hurt to another person helps us move beyond any feelings of guilt, responsibility, or embarrassment at having been betrayed. This is especially helpful when we are able to verbalize our hurt to a person who has or is going through the same thing.

One of the most humiliating things that can happen to career people today is something called "downsizing." Regardless of the name, the bottom line is the same. Our company no longer wants us. Our position has been eliminated, or they may call it early retirement. We perceive it as being fired. We are no longer needed or wanted. In extreme cases, our positions are eliminated just prior to our eligibility for retirement.

In many communities there are "employment support groups" for those who find themselves in this position. Often, the members of these groups are individuals who have given their lives to the same company. I remember visiting one such group and hearing stories of professionals who had brought their companies multi-million dollar deals on the same day that they were given their pink slips. They were then turned out into the world. They perceived themselves as too old and overqualified. Beginning again did not appear to be an option.

The sense of hurt and betrayal for these individuals can be paralyzing. The humiliation and embarrassment can be overwhelming. In the support groups they come together with others who understand this hurt because they too have been injured. I remember one of the members of such a group explaining their purpose to me. "In this group," he explained, "we are able to let go of the hurt that could potentially anchor us in our misery. By listening to each other, we help each other find the strength to move forward. We have all accepted the fact that in this life **pain is inevitable, but misery is optional.**"

"IT IS NOT YOUR FAULT"

We are able to reveal our pain to another human being when we are able to accept our own humanity. If we insist on maintaining the illusion that we are always in control, that we are invincible, we will not be able to talk about our pain. If preserving our own illusion that our marriage is perfect, our spouse is perfect, our children are beyond rebellion, and our employer and/or employees are beyond reproach we will not be able to share our grief with anyone.

It is not unusual for a person to blame themselves for being a victim or target of another's sin. We feel foolish for having trusted the person. We then have a difficult time forgiving ourselves for having trusted. We have a difficult time forgiving ourselves for the sins committed by a trusted spouse, employee, employer, or friend. This is a tangled web.

The acceptance of our humanity is a critical component in the process of forgiving. Sin is possible precisely because we are human beings. We are human and those who hurt us are human. As long as we maintain the illusion that we are beyond being hurt by another, forgiveness is not possible. Such an illusion will bring only bitterness toward the other and contempt toward ourselves.

Indeed, it will be a rare person who is not tempted to blame themselves for being a victim or target of another's sin. "How could I have been so stupid... so blind... so naive?" Most of us will feel foolish for having trusted the person who hurt us. We will then have a difficult time forgiving ourselves for having trusted. We will have a difficult time forgiving ourselves for someone else's sins. The web becomes even more tangled.

In the extreme, there are those who will feel a sense of shame about themselves. Shame means that there is something wrong with them. They feel abasement so strongly that they reason that they are completely unworthy of love. They erroneously believe they are deserving of the pain and punishment that has been inflicted on them. They are only getting what they deserve. We have to get outside these feelings in order to get a healthy perspective.

It is important that we understand that we did nothing wrong when we trusted another person. This is an important learning if are ever going to be able to trust again. We must not judge, belittle, or punish ourselves for trusting. When we choose to trust, that is positive information about us. When our trust is betrayed, that is revealing information about the one who chose to hurt us.

By talking about the hurt that another has brought upon us, we can come to terms with the behavior of those who hurt us. **We need to say to ourselves over and over that their behavior is not information about us. Their behavior is information about them!** If our spouse chooses to be sexually unfaithful to us, this is not information about us. It is not even information about our marriage. It is information about the way our spouse has chosen to behave. It is information about them. It is important for us to acknowledge that they had other choices, but they chose instead to betray us. Once we are able to work through our hurt, we are in a more healthy position to make our own choices about them and our marriage. If we strike out from our own hurt, we may make choices that we would later regret.

DON'T GET STUCK TALKING ABOUT YOUR PAIN

The man invited me to have lunch with him. I could tell he was an individual carrying a lot of hurt. His countenance was very controlled. He spoke through gritted teeth. He shook his head and breathed heavily when other drivers, pedestrians, or waiters did anything that displeased him. His words were carefully chosen. His every movement was intentional. He immediately registered on my radar screen as an angry individual.

I listened with great compassion as he began to tell me about the hurt in his life. He described it in graphic detail. I could not believe the insensitivity that had been shown him. I could not believe that another human being could be so cruel to someone that they had professed to love. I was just on the verge of affirming his anger when it hit me. He was describing an event that happened over thirty years ago! Yet, he was describing it with such fervor and passion, I had first thought it had occurred just a few days ago.

I observed the impact that thirty years of anger and hurt had taken on this man. His face was contorted with the pain. He looked much older than his years. I wondered what all this hate was doing to his vital organs. I was getting a pretty good idea of what it was doing to his relationships. No one could do anything right. He had something negative to say about most every significant person in his life. I knew it would just be a matter of time until I would be added to his list. He would be equally disapproving of me.

It did not surprise me to discover that this man considered himself to be a very religious person. In his words, he was "proud to be a follower of Jesus." He had little use for the "bleeding hearts" that were out to destroy the Church. He believed every word of the Bible and he looked forward to having a priest who would preach the scriptures to the people. Of course, he had cut his pledge to the parish because "he had no use for the last rector. He was just too liberal. The people need to have the Bible preached to them!" He pounded on the table. He wanted to make sure that I planned to tell the people the truth. They needed to repent of their sins and "get right with the Lord." As for all the liberal bishops in the Episcopal Church, he would gladly "take them out one by one."

As might be predicted, he had some equally unflattering words for people of color, gays and lesbians, Roman Catholics, Jews, the attendants in the local food marts, and all people living on welfare. When our meal was served, he bowed his head and said grace over the meal in a voice audible enough to distract the diners at the nearby tables. I could not help but recall the words of Jonathan Swift, "Just enough religion to hate, not enough to love."

There was a moment of light relief for me during the meal. My luncheon companion had sent his soup back to the kitchen at least twice. He had been less than kind to the waiter. He then began to harass the waiter demanding to know just where his soup was. The waiter held his own with the man. "Sir," he stated. "There are only two people in this restaurant who even care where your soup is. You need to know that one of them is rapidly losing interest!"

When we walk into our pain, we also must take care not to get stuck there. While we can make the observation that no one dies from the pain itself, we can let the pain destroy our souls. The pain can take away our ability to enjoy life. It can fixate us in such a fashion that the event itself becomes our constant companion. It becomes something that we rehearse over and over again. Each time we rehearse the event, the pain is given new energy and new life. We can become frozen in "analysis paralysis." We simply continue to spread our venom everywhere we go. Each time we find another willing set of ears our bitterness does not get negated; to the contrary, it gets renewed and it grows.

When we get fixated in the trauma of an event, the walls that we surround ourselves with grow thick and restrictive. We lose our ability to be spontaneous, open, creative, and flexible. We lose our sense of humor. Our anger gets transferred onto anyone we perceive as different from us or who disagrees with us. Life is no longer something to be enjoyed, but a burden to bear. Love is not life-giving, but a duty. Our faith loses its ability to give us spiritual energy and becomes a rigid religiosity that must be defended and forced onto others.

CHOOSE A LISTENER WHO WILL HOLD US ACCOUNTABLE

I have often thought about that man. I wish that he had opened his grief up to a friend who would have challenged him to move through the forgiveness process and not get stuck. I wish that he had trusted a member of the clergy or another member of the helping professions. I can't help but wonder how his life would be different today. He was obviously a very talented man, but what a waste. Now, because of his bitterness, he had become someone to avoid. I repeat, martyrs make lousy party guests!

MARTYRS MAKE LOUSY PARTY GUESTS!

A friend or professional can also keep us out of the sand trap of developing lightning rods for all of life's ills. If a parent or other authority figure has betrayed us, we may spend our lives suspicious of all authority figures. They become the lightning rods for our unresolved hurt. Likewise, if a member of the opposite sex has broken our trust, we reason, "all of them are the same." I have known men and women who just don't understand why they can't find a life partner. Yet, their conversations often reveal unresolved hurts that continue to serve as obstacles to building any intimacy.

In the same way, much of the anti-clericalism in religion can find its origin in the unresolved anger an individual may be nursing against God. They hold God responsible for their pain. Any symbol of God then becomes an acceptable target for that anger. It is so sad to see the people who cannot develop a relationship with God, a member of the clergy or a faith community because of a past hurt or disappointment in one of God's representatives.

I find it interesting that over the past thirty-four years of parish ministry my life has been threatened on four occasions. Each time threats have come with quotes from the Bible. The Christians issuing the threats used the scriptures to justify labeling me as unacceptable. They used their every creative bone to question my spirituality and my integrity. It has been important for me to keep these threats in perspective. Again, these are not information about me. I am confident that at least two of them were the result of forgiveness issues that had never been resolved. These individuals needed to forgive another who had hurt them. I question whether or not the real issue was that they needed to forgive themselves. They found most unacceptable in me that which they despised in themselves.

It is imperative that we share our pain with someone who can help us. They must do more than just lend a sympathetic ear and validate our hurt. They need to be able to help us get the betrayal into a framework that we can work through. The person we choose to open our grief to needs to hold us accountable to move through this phase of the forgiveness process. They need to encourage us to use the pain itself as a learning experience. We need to take the time to pause, reflect, and process what has happened to us. We need to be in a healthy position to decide how we are going to respond to the perpetrator of the hurt and the hurt itself. We do not want to simply react or strike out. Our response needs to be thoughtful and intentional.

When we choose to forgive the people who have hurt us our spirits can be released from the torments that imprison them. By verbalizing our pain to an active listener who will hold us accountable, we are in a better position to make the decision to forgive. They can listen to us with their heart while keeping us from becoming stuck in the talking phase of the forgiveness process. Hearing ourselves describe our pain, embarrassment, and humiliation to such a listener will be a monumental step in the process of forgiving and getting our lives back.

Questions for Reflection and/or Action

1. Why is it important for us to accept our own humanity in order to forgive?

2. How is not talking about our hurt with another person a form of denial?

3. Who do you know that you can share your grief with? Will they hold you accountable? Will they keep you from getting stuck?

4. Do you think it is possible to truly forgive without hearing yourself verbalize the depth of your hurt and humiliation to another?

STEP THREE

"DO GET ANGRY"

When a person has been hurt, anger is a natural response. The desire to strike out at the person who has hurt them is overwhelming. Anger can be expressed in a healthy or an unhealthy way. When it is unhealthy it does not hurt the object of our anger. To the contrary, unhealthy anger destroys us. We become victims over and over again.

If I step on your foot, it will hurt. Unless you have been trained in some misplaced version of courtesy, you will respond by asking me to get off your foot. If I ignore your request and continue to put pressure on your foot or repeatedly step on it, you will get angry. The anger is a natural response to hurt. When another person has invaded our space, violated our trust, or otherwise stepped on our hearts, it will make us angry. Anger is a part of our created order. God created us with the ability to get angry.

It is quite easy to observe the inherent nature of anger. Simply stand at the window of a newborn nursery. When those who are just hours old are not fed, changed, or otherwise attended to, they get angry and they let everyone around them know it. No one teaches an infant how to be angry. Anger is a natural response to an unfriendly environment.

The classical case of anger can be seen in the scriptures when Jesus made a whip of cords in order to chase the moneychangers out of the temple.* The priests and the moneychangers of the day had taken the temple sacrifices for sin and turned them into a form of greed and corruption. When Jesus witnessed the injustice, he grew very angry and he took action. His anger motivated him to do something about the injustice being forced on the common people. This is an example of a healthy expression of anger. The anger is not used to attack a person, but to attack an injustice.

When I lived in Houston, Texas I became familiar with the work of a woman by the name of Pam Lychner. She was the founder of an organization in Texas known as "Justice for All." This organization, which now is in virtually every state in the union, is an advocacy group for victims of crimes. Pam created the organization in response to a traumatic experience in her own life.

Pam and her husband Joe renovated houses in the Houston area and then placed them on the market for sale. One particular afternoon a man called Pam and asked her to show him one of the houses they had for sale. When Pam arrived to show the man the house, he attacked her. The man did not know that Joe also came with Pam. When he heard Pam screaming he ran to her aid. The two of them were able to overpower the man and to lock the man in a closet until the police arrived. The man was found guilty of the charges against him and was sent to prison.

From prison, however, the man employed an attorney and sued the Lychners for pain and suffering from being locked in

---

* Matthew 21:12ff

the closet until the police arrived. Pam turned her anger in on herself. She became very depressed and was unable to even leave her home for great periods of time. Several months later, however, Pam redirected her anger. She directed her anger into action. She went to the Texas State Legislature and formed the advocacy group known as "Justice for All." Pam used her anger to accomplish a notable task. I share this story with you as yet one further example of the way that anger can motivate us to correct a wrong and accomplish a great good.

> **IF WE DENY THE ANGER AND BURY IT, WE DO NOT BURY IT DEAD, WE BURY IT ALIVE. IT WILL MULTIPLY AND IT WILL BECOME GANGRENOUS. IT MAY EXPRESS ITSELF PHYSICALLY.**

UNHEALTHY ANGER

There are numerous unhealthy ways we can express our anger. Most will end up leading to our own self destruction. One that we discussed earlier is assuming the role of the martyr. This often happens when a person gets stuck in the talking phase of forgiveness. Because of what someone else did to us, no one will ever be able to blame us. Our cause is "holy" and our bitterness justified. We are entitled to wrap ourselves in a hard shell of bitterness and snap at any one who does not take "our side" against the outcasts.

We can also use our anger as an excuse to "get even" with those who have hurt us. In a marriage, a single act of adultery on the part of one spouse can lead to multiple acts of adultery on the part of the other. These acts are justified in the name of revenge or evening the score. I remember visiting with one man that had caught his wife in an act of adultery. He justified his multiple "one night stands", often with his wife's friends and acquaintances, on the grounds that she owed him. He told me, "I do not believe in getting angry. I believe in getting even!" He shared with me that before his wife's act of adultery he had been completely faithful to her for twelve years. He asserted that he had not so much as flirted with another woman. Since discovering that his wife had been unfaithful he had committed exactly 87 acts of adultery over two years with 87 different women. When I pushed him on just how many illicit sexual acts it would take to even the score with his wife, his response was "a lot more than 87."

When a person hurts us we will respond by being angry. This is natural. God has wired us to respond to injustice with anger. However, we need to choose to respond in a healthy fashion. Sometimes, people choose to take the anger out on themselves. There are so many physical manifestations that may be attributed in part to buried anger. The possibilities include hyedal hernias, shoulder and back pain, migraine headaches, and colitis. The psychophysical expressions can be even more serious. Anger turned in on ourselves can also manifest itself in depression, heart disease, blood pressure problems; even some forms of cancer in some patients may find their source in buried anger.

I am not suggesting that these diseases always find their origin in repressed anger. There are many contributing factors to any illness. The observation I want to make is that each of us has one or more pre-dispositions to certain illnesses. Some of us may be more genetically susceptible to certain diseases. Repressed anger may just be the fire needed to light the particular fuse in our body.

Many people who have explosive tempers are folks who have suppressed their anger. Typically they are people who do not document their anger when it occurs. Rather, they choose to swallow it or set their jaw. They are not unlike the collectors of the old S&H Green Stamp Books. Stamps were awarded when a person made a purchase. The stamps were placed in the book and when the book was full, a person could turn the book in for a prize. People who swallow their anger are like those collecting stamps. Only, sooner or later, some poor unsuspecting person is going to give them the last stamp. Then, they get to cash in all their saved-up anger on that one person. This is why their anger, once expressed, is so far out of proportion to the offense.

Socially, buried anger may manifest itself in sexual promiscuity, the physical cutting of the body, overspending, and chemical abuse. Many extramarital affairs can be attributed to suppressed anger. So can acts of theft from employees, parents, or friends. "I deserve this. They owe me." In the extreme, homicide and suicide may also find their genesis in unexpressed anger. The research is yet to be concluded, but I have read of some studies suggesting that these behaviors or misbehaviors might also be genetically influenced. How one expresses one's anger is a matter of choice to be sure. The choice itself, however, may have more to do with heredity than environment. Therefore, it is imperative that we be in touch with our anger.

IF POSSIBLE, WE NEED TO CONFRONT OUR OFFENDER

When another person has stepped on our heart we need to express our anger in a healthy fashion. By far the healthiest thing that we can do is tell the person who has hurt us. Our focus must be on our pain and not on them or their action. Name-calling, verbal abuse, or any other verbal attack on them is not helpful. They need to see our hurt and anger. They need to hear our hurt and anger. We need to be able to tell them just how their actions have hurt us and made us angry.

If we simply dismiss their behavior and not insist that they see and hear our pain, we become participants in their betrayal. We become co-conspirators with them in their misbehavior. We become their willing victims. Those who have hurt us need to hear our pain. They need to come to terms with the depth of our injury. Hurting us is one of the consequences of their actions. It is a consequence they must face in order for their own experience of forgiveness to be complete.

IF WE DO NOT HOLD THEM ACCOUNTABLE FOR THEIR BEHAVIOR, WE IN ESSENCE, GIVE THEM PERMISSION TO BEHAVE IN THE SAME WAY AGAIN.

Those who have injured us need to hear and see our hurt. No one can do this for us. We are the only ones who can verbalize our anguish and our humiliation. If we minimize it or dismiss it, they will dismiss it as well. However, we must understand that when we bury our pain, we do not bury it dead. We bury it alive. It will return!

In one parish I served there had been a trusted business manager for many years. When I became rector of the parish I became suspicious of the business manager's accounting. When I organized an internal investigation with some of the lay leaders I trusted, the business manager turned the tables. He used other church officials to launch a counter-attack against me and the leaders that I had asked to assist me in the investigation. It became very brutal. The lay leaders I chose to assist me and I were subjected to character assassinations, suggestions, and accusations directed at our own credibility.

Ultimately, we prevailed and my suspicions were confirmed. That business manager pleaded guilty to the charges brought against him by the legal authorities. He is currently serving his sentence in the penitentiary. The lay leaders who had assisted me and I were invited to make statements at the sentencing hearing. We all went. It was the first time that we had come face to face with the business manager since the day that we confronted him with the evidence of his malfeasance almost one year earlier. While the man has never issued a word of apology to any of us, we each found it extremely cathartic to be able to express our hurt, disappointment and anger directly to him. It did much for our own healing. It has also given me a clearer perspective on the need for victims to be able to confront those who have injured them.

> **WHEN WE EXPRESS OUR ANGER, WE DISCHARGE IT.**
> **WE GET RID OF IT.**

I remember listening to the story of a woman whose twelve-year old son had been murdered. Even though the murderer had been caught and sentenced to death, she could not release the hurt. She had become emotionally paralyzed. Her depression had literally put her in the bed for months at a time. She could not stop blaming herself. She reasoned that she should have been there for her son. She wanted to believe that she could have done something to help him. She directed her hurt, grief, and anger on herself. She was holding herself responsible for her son's murder. In a very real way, this murderer had killed two people. He had taken the life of both the woman and her son.

The woman's physician convinced the prison authorities to allow her to confront the man who had taken her son's life. The man agreed to meet with the woman just a few weeks before his execution. It was not until the woman was able to confront her son's killer and verbalize her anger and hurt that she was able to even begin to get her life back. She visited the man several times before he was executed. The visits were filled with pain. On each visit, the man listened and asked the woman's forgiveness. The initial confrontations were filled with negative emotions. She was unable to utter the words of absolution. However, each successive visit became less and less hurtful. As she released her pain, the woman was able to respond positively to the man's tearful pleas for forgiveness. In doing so, she got her life back. By confronting the consequences of his behavior, the criminal found release as well.

Depending on the depth of the hurt and betrayal, we may not discharge all of our anger during the first encounter. A few hours or days may pass and we will find that we need to let them hear our hurt again. The purpose is not to let them "have it." The purpose is to let them "hear us." Our goal is not to hurt them. To borrow the old cliché, "two wrongs do not make a right." Our purpose is to express our hurt, our disappointment, and yes, our anger. Therefore, it is imperative that we be in touch with our anger.

SOMETIMES IT IS NOT POSSIBLE TO PERSONALLY CONFRONT THE PERSON

It is sad, but true that some folks will never apologize. They will never ask us to forgive them. On occasion, this is simply not a possibility. I remember counseling a young woman whose father had committed suicide. She had never really known him. He deserted the family when she was just three years old. The man had left her mother for another woman. That marriage did not last but a couple of years. He then moved to the opposite coast of the United States. The girl basically grew up without her father. When she was nineteen the man moved back to the West Coast and tried to re-enter her life. They we just beginning to get to know one another when for some reason yet to be explained, the man ended his life.

For fifteen years the girl, now a woman, had gone from one short-term relationship to another. She was unable to make a commitment to any man, even though she had actually been engaged to be married twice. She cancelled each wedding just weeks short of the scheduled dates. In the same way, she had been unable to maintain a stable employment situation. She gained incredible amounts of weight and started a program of piercing her various body parts. She came to me in a deep depression.

Over the weeks her story unfolded, it became clear to me that the only way this young woman was going to get her life back was to make the decision to forgive her father. When I confronted her with the thought that the reason she was unable to enjoy the present and commit to the future was because she was still anchored to the past, her initial reaction was denial. I suggested that she needed to forgive her father. She shouted back, "You have got to be kidding? He deserted me. I never knew the man. I'll never forgive him!"

I asked her if she had ever visited the place that her father was buried. She blurted back, "Why would I do that?" I countered that if she was serious about getting over her depression perhaps a visit to her father's grave was in order. I told her that I would go with her. I wanted her to confront her father with her hurt and her pain. With some reluctance she agreed.

When we arrived at the place his ashes had been interred, she sat down on the grass. She began to cry. I encouraged her to tell her father about her hurt, her anger, and her feelings of betrayal. The pain gushed out of her even more forcefully than I had hoped it would.

For over an hour, she pounded her fists on his grave. She shouted at him, talking, crying, and demanding answers from him. Her body shook with emotion. There would be moments of calm, followed by yet more eruptions. Like an angry volcano that had been building a lethal pressure for years, she exploded. Then came the moment of quiet sobbing. She managed a gentle smile. She patted the ground and uttered, "I forgive you Daddy. I don't understand why you did what you did. I wish things could have been different between us. I love you Daddy. I'll not bother you again. Rest in peace." With that, she stood up, hugged my neck and wept just a bit longer. Then she looked back at the spot one final time. She took my hand and led me away from the grave.

That experience was pivotal for that woman. She began to grow in grace. She went back to school and got a degree in her chosen profession. The weight began to fall off her body and her soul. She once again took pride in her appearance. At this writing she is engaged to be married. This time, I don't think she will run.

Visiting the grave of someone who has hurt us is one way of releasing our anger when a direct confrontation is not possible. On occasion, a letter or series of letters that are written but never mailed can help us discharge our anger. I have been a part of services in which the participants wrote forgiveness messages on slips of paper and then attached them to helium filled balloons. These were released into the heavens. On a couple of occasions, I have accompanied priests back to parishes that had been particularly cruel to them. Quite literally we paraded around the parish property literally shaking the dust of the place off our feet. We would walk around and around until all the anger was vented and replaced with humor, laughter, and then finally release.

It is important that we not take the anger out on ourselves. It is critical that we express our anger in a healthy fashion. If confronting the person who has hurt us is a healthy and possible option we need to exercise it. If confronting them is not a healthy option nor a realistic possibility then we need to consider other methods for doing so. The goal is not to put them on the spot. It is not to embarrass or humiliate them. The goal is to have the opportunity to discharge the poison that is infecting our souls.

Confronting the Person May Not Be Enough

As I have stated and will continue to emphasize, forgiveness is a process. Confronting the person who has betrayed us and expressing our anger directly to the person who hurt us may not be enough. We may need to release our anger again and again before it is completely alleviated. As long as we have even a small remnant of resentment toward the other in our hearts, forgiveness will not be complete. We may may need to ventilate with a counselor, clergy person, or trusted advisor who can guide us through the process and keep the expression of our anger healthy.

There is one more aspect to the healing process. We need to become even more physically active when our heart has been hurt. We need to walk, run, shout, beat a pillow, kick a punching bag, or anything that can help us discharge the anger. When we feel the hurt and anger washing over us, don't allow it to drag us down. Don't let it drive us to food or chemical abuse. Get some exercise!

Discharging Anger is a Three-fold Process

Discharging our anger is a three-fold process. It requires us to express it directly to the person who has hurt us. It may also require us to ventilate to a sympathetic professional. And it requires us to get some exercise. Of course, the process of ventilating anger is different for each individual. Some may talk more. Others may exercise more. The important part of the process is to acknowledge the anger and then find a healthy way to discharge it.

As we have already suggested, ignoring or burying our anger may have devastating consequences on our physical, mental, and spiritual health. To even suggest that we can have someone walk on our hearts and not respond with anger is ridiculous. God has wired us to respond to pain with anger.

Again, the Bible teaches us to "Be angry, but do not sin."* Anger as a response to hurt and betrayal is a God-given emotion. Expressing that anger is a necessary part of the forgiveness process. It is required for our healing. The anger itself can serve as a motivator to help us right wrongs and build better relationships, marriages, and work environments, even a better world. These are all good and healthy expressions of anger.

However, if we use our anger to belittle another person, even if is the person who has hurt us, is wrong. To verbally or physically abuse another person with our anger is wrong. To allow our anger to lead us to slander or attack the character of another is equally wrong. Our anger must never become a weapon that we use against another. God did not give us anger to use as a club to beat each other up.

When expressing our anger, we need to focus on "I" statements. "I feel ...I hurt ... I am humiliated.... I am embarrassed... I am angry." Avoid the "you statements." This is not the time to focus on their behavior. It is not a time for blame. It is not a time for judgment, labeling, or name-calling.

Even if a catastrophic event or accident is causing our pain, the expression of our anger is required for healing. Sometimes our anger needs to be directed at God. Shaking our fists at the heavens can be very therapeutic. I remember one woman telling me that she was so angry with God that she was refusing to talk with the Almighty. She had decided to go to a higher authority.

---

* Ephesians 4:26

"I am so angry with God," she exclaimed, "I have decided to go directly to his Mother!"

In order to ventilate our anger, we have to get in touch with our anger. The only way that can be done is to talk about how we feel. Analyzing the other or trying to understand why they did what they did does not help us document our hurt. "You statements" only lead to an escalating combat. They will invariably put the other person on the defensive or worse, the offensive. Healing begins by verbalizing our own feelings.

"You statements" are like pouring gasoline on an already blazing fire. They only feed our anger. They escalate the tension. Moreover, they can detour us from using our anger to improve our relationship. The ultimate goal is to get our life back. "I statements" have the ability to set us free from our hurt, resentment and bitterness.

The great danger is that if we begin to nurture our anger with "you statements," this will only serve to turn our expressions of hurt to resentment. Bitterness is but a short walk from resentment. Once bitterness is achieved, we can get stuck. The forgiveness process has been frozen in time. There will be no healing for ourselves or anyone else. There will be no reconciliation. There will be no restoration. There will just be a lifetime of reruns. We will continually play the hurts of the past in all of our tomorrows.

We have to guard against getting stuck in the anger phase of the forgiveness process. Once we get stuck in our misery, getting our lives back will prove even more difficult.

I think often about the statement that the man made in the employment support group. **"In life pain is inevitable, but misery is optional."** We have all known people who have chosen misery over life. Their hurts are their badges of dishonor. They wear them proudly. They speak of them often. Sadly, they also often use them as justification for bringing misery upon others. Therefore, it is imperative that we be in touch with our anger.

Verbalizing our hurt and anger the first few times will not be easy. Expressing our anger will expose the depth of our hurt. Likewise, confronting our betrayer may cause us to experience the pain again and again, but those who have hurt us need to see our tears. If we attempt to bury our anger, we need to be reminded again that we will not bury it dead. We will bury it alive and it will become a bitter poison to our souls and all that our lives touch.

Poet William Blake reminds us that if we retain our anger and allow it to grow, it will become murderous.

A Poison Tree

I was angry with my friend:
I told my wrath, my wrath did end.
I was angry with my foe:
I told it not, my wrath did grow.

And I watered it in fears,
Night and morning with my tears;
And I sunned it with smiles,
And with soft, deceitful wiles.

And it grew both day and night,
Till it bore an apple bright;
And my foe beheld it shine,
And he knew that it was mine.

And into my garden stole,
When the night had veiled the pole:
In the morning glad I see
My foe outstretched beneath the tree.

QUESTIONS FOR REFLECTIONS AND/OR ACTION

1. What is your usual method for dealing with anger? Is it healthy?

2. Who do you know that will let you ventilate your anger with them, but keep you from getting stuck?

3. How would it feel to confront the person with your anger? Rehearse in your mind what you want to say to them. Use "I" statements. Avoid attacking them.

4. What physical exercise or activity can you begin or enhance which will help you discharge your anger?

5. What are some other things you can do for yourself to help you get through your anger? Yoga? Massage? Support Group? Other?

Step Four

"Forgiving and Forgetting"

We are not wired to develop amnesia. As much as we may want to forget the trauma it will always remain with us. We can recall the full force of the hurt in an instant. We cannot forget, but we can choose not to remember.

"Forgive and forget" is a phrase that sounds awfully hollow when we are hurting. It reminds me of the cartoon of the elderly man dressed in his confederate uniform waving the confederate flag. The caption reads, "Forget – Never!" When your heart has literally been ripped from your chest the suggestion that you suddenly develop amnesia is not a very attractive alternative. Rather than forget, the first temptation is to make sure that you don't forget, that the person who has hurt you doesn't forget, and if possible make sure that everyone they know never forgets just what kind of person they truly are.

When I was in the seventh grade, all male students were required to take a course in woodworking in our school. On the first day of school, we were handed a full typewritten page containing the ten steps for bringing a piece of lumber to square.

The shop teacher advised us that we had two weeks to memorize this sheet of paper. We would then be required to reproduce it for him, word for word, without any error. If we failed to do so at the end of the two weeks, we would each receive one swat to our posteriors from the wooden paddle that he had hanging behind his desk. He then took the wooden paddle down and fondled it. Obviously, he had taken great pride in bringing it to perfect square.

He then announced that if on the second day we failed to perfectly repeat the procedure we would receive two swats. On the third day three swats would be delivered and so forth until we all were able to recite the procedure without error.

Predictably on the appointed day, not all the boys were able to repeat the process without error. So one by one, they went to the head of the class. In front of their fellow classmates, they were instructed to bend over and grab their ankles. The shop teacher then administered the appropriate motivation.

I have often thought of just how humiliating that experience was for my fellow students. I have also thought of how it exemplifies Christianity at its worst. It has been said that the Church of Jesus Christ is the only army on earth that shoots its wounded. The church at its worst chooses to deal with sinners using the shop teacher's theology. The best deterrent is to brand all adulterers with the scarlet letter. Hold the sinner up to the light of public humiliation. Let them be an example. Publicly shame, humiliate, embarrass, and punish them. Then everyone else will think twice before getting out of line. With such an attitude we are but a breath away from the Salem Witch Trials.

The sad truth is that when we attempt to punish another for their sins against us through humiliation or any means, we are forced to relive the hurt and the experience all over again. Each act of revenge brings forward the memory of the hurt and the pain all over again. The video in our minds hits replay over and over again.

> ## THE GOAL IS TO TURN OFF THE RE-RUNS.

"REVENGE THROUGH HUMILIATION"

Since the Church itself often chooses to make a public spectacle of those who have fallen from grace, it only makes sense that would be our temptation as well. I would like to suggest that we not confuse forgiveness with making a public spectacle out of those who stumble and fall. We do not have to make the sins of those who have offended us fodder for the town gossips in order to find the strength and grace to forgive them. Public humiliation and embarrassment of the offender have more to do with revenge and mean-spiritedness than they do with forgiveness. When we make the decision to forgive, we also make the decision not to seek revenge. If we choose revenge, an eye for an eye, we end up continuing in the pain. The goal of forgiving is to move beyond the pain and get our lives back. We can forgive those who have hurt us without holding them up to the public eye.

When Jesus instructed us to confront those that were in sin he told us to first do so in secret. The purpose was not to embarrass or humiliate but to redeem. By allowing the person their dignity we would not only retain our brother or sister, but would retain our relationship with them and they could be brought to repentance. Jesus further instructed that if they then would not listen to us and remained unrepentant we should take two or three witnesses with us. Still, the goal is to bring them to repentance. It is only when the person remains totally unrepentant that we identify them before the entire congregation.

They are identified not for the purposes of a public stoning, but to insure that the innocent may not fall victim to their wiles.

"ACTIONS HAVE CONSEQUENCES"

It is important at this point to make a point of clarification. Jesus calls Christians to be in the forgiveness business. I am arguing that the only way that you can get through your current hurt and begin again is to be in the forgiveness business as well. Having made that statement, it needs to be clarified that the state and the federal government are not in the forgiveness business! **While most all criminal acts are a sin, not all sins are defined as criminal acts by the State.** When we speak of forgiveness, we are treating sin as a disease that needs to be healed. We are not talking about crimes that mandate punishment by the State. The consequences of criminal behavior cannot be escaped, but the truth of the matter is that we will all suffer silently or publicly the consequences of our sins as well.

During seminary, I shared in a ministry with the Episcopal chaplain to Statesville Prison in Joliet, Illinois. My charge was to work with small groups of prisoners. Their song was so predictable. "The state has taken away my freedom." They would whine, "How can the state do such a thing?" Our task was to try to instill in them a sense of responsibility. We tried to help them understand that actions have consequences. If you take a revolver and walk into a service station to steal the cash from the attendant, you have made a life decision. You have made the decision to forfeit your freedom. You have made the decision to go to prison. No one took anything away from you. You made the decision yourself. **Actions have consequences. Forgiveness cannot change that reality.**

Forgiveness does not relieve us of the consequences of our actions. When we violate the laws of the state, there will be consequences. When we violate our marriage vows, there will be consequences. When we violate the commandments of God, there will be consequences. Even if our sins remain secret, we will suffer the consequences of our actions. Others may not be aware of our sin against them, but any person with a sense of right and wrong will be aware of the wrong they have done. Living with unrepentant sins comes at a price to us. Our relationships with those we have hurt will suffer. Our own physical, mental, and emotional health will suffer. We will suffer spiritually.

"Forgiveness Takes Time"

If we are to truly forgive another person, we must have a change of heart toward that person. Depending on the depth of the hurt, it will take time. We must not berate ourselves or think we are less faithful or spiritual because we cannot achieve a change of heart overnight. While all Christians need to be quick to utter the words of absolution, we must recognize that just saying the words does not make them an emotional reality. To forgive someone who has hurt us may be a heart-wrenching experience. Forgiveness does not remove the consequences of their behavior. They must continue to live with those consequences. We often have to live not only with the consequences of their actions, but the pain, **and the memory** as well.

I repeat - forgiving another person is a spiritual process requiring Divine assistance. In order to forgive, we often must live through long sleepless nights. The grief in our hearts will bring unexpected and wrenching tears to our eyes. Just when we think that we have forgiven the person and put the past behind us, the memory of it will rush over us like a giant tsunami. Weeks, even months, may pass with no thought of the hurt.

Then, out of nowhere, the pain will wash over us, as piercing as though it had just happened.

Sometimes the memory will be stimulated by an event, an associating date or place. On other occasions it might be an odor, a song, a movie, or a story. Ordinarily it will be some symbol that was associated with the painful event. Those who struggle with forgiving deep betrayals are no strangers to waking up in the middle of the night in a cold sweat with tears rolling down their cheeks. They are no strangers to reoccurring nightmares in which the event is either acted out again or symbolically acted out for us. The accompanying pain again rips at the broken places in the heart.

Forgiving takes time. Sometimes it takes a long time to heal. Still, we must forgive those who have hurt us even if they do not ask our forgiveness. We must forgive them for our own soul's health. We must forgive them so that we can return to a place of wholeness and get on with our lives.

"LEAVE THE PAST IN THE PAST"

While we may not recover all the positive feelings we once felt about the person who has hurt us, we still must let go of the event. We must let go of the past. We must leave the event behind us. We need to move forward. We need to let go of the feelings of revenge and resentment. Let me repeat, this is not easy, but we must do it in order to help ourselves.

I am reminded of the farmer who had a cat that he loved ever so dearly. To the farmer's great grief, the cat died. The farmer gave the cat a proper burial in the flower garden behind his house. However, this burial was unique. The farmer buried the cat, but he left the tail sticking out of the ground. A week or so passed and the farmer began to think about his cat. He decided to go to the burial site to check on the cat. He reached down, grabbed the tail, and pulled the cat out of the ground. He looked at the cat. The cat did not look so well. The cat did not smell very good either. The farmer returned the cat to his resting place, but again, he left the tail sticking out. Each time the farmer went to the grave and pulled the cat out of the ground, the cat looked worse and smelled worse then it did on the previous viewing.

It is the same way with our past hurts. As painful as they were at the time, each time we bring them into the present for another viewing, they look worse and they smell worse. In short, they hurt even more than they did initially. When we forgive another, whether we reconcile with them or not, we must leave the past in the past. This is what it means to forgive and forget. It does not mean we develop amnesia. We will never be able to erase the painful offense from our memory. However, if we are to forgive and forget we must bury the event in the past, tail and all.

Turning off the video is one of the greatest gifts that we can give ourselves. As long as we keep the video going, we will continue to suffer and agonize over the event. If we allow our minds to follow the hurtful course, we will relive the painful moment over and over again. While we will never forget it, we can turn off the re-runs. We can choose to leave the event and all the surrounding details, real and imagined, in the past.

If we are going to let go of the feelings of resentment and revenge, we must leave the past in the past and not bring it into the present. When we leave the past in the past and not carry it into the present, we set ourselves free from replaying the experience so that we can move forward with our own lives. It bears repeating, to forgive those who have hurt us is a gift. It just may be one of the best gifts that we can give ourselves. A critical part of the gift that we can forgive ourselves is to make the conscious decision to leave the past in the past. We make the decision to bury the painful event in yesterday. When we bury it, we choose to bury it, tail and all.

QUESTIONS FOR REFLECTION AND/OR ACTION

1. What are some specific things that you can do to leave the past in the past? Are there symbols or hurtful reminders that you need to remove from your possession? Would removing those things help you leave the past in the past?

2. What are some of the things you can do to help yourself be patient with the process of forgiving and forgetting?

3. Do you understand that when you attempt to humiliate or embarrass the person who has offended you that you actively bring the past forward, give it more life? In what ways will you suffer the consequences of their actions yet one more time?

4. Can you make the distinction in your mind between forgiveness and "actions that have consequences"?

5. In the space below make three sketches. Have one sketch depict the happiest time in your life, the second the saddest time in your life and the third, where you are right now. Where do you want to live the rest of your life? What do you need to do to get there?

STEP FIVE

"CHOOSE TO RECONCILE"

Before we can reconcile with another we have to know that they are truly sorry. We need to hear their words of repentance. We need to know that their contrition is genuine. To reconcile with those who are not truly contrite is to give them permission to hurt us again.

Forgiving those who have hurt us is a process that involves several choices. One of the most difficult of those choices is to reconcile with the person that has offended us. Here again the choice before us is really quite clear. We can either nurture the hurt and bitterness that ultimately will destroy us and those around us. Or, we can forgive the person, put the past behind us, and live into a future free of the pain. The question at this point is whether or not the person who has hurt us will be a continuing part of that future.

Reconciliation requires that both people want an ongoing and newly defined relationship. But how can we be sure that the one who has hurt us really wants to reconcile with us? How can we be sure that they are genuinely sorry for what they did? Just what emotions, feelings, and changes in behavior should we look for in the person that has offended us before we make the decision to reconcile with them? How can we know that they are truly sincere when they ask our forgiveness? How can we be certain that they are not just playing us for a fool or wanting to avoid the consequences of their actions when they appeal to us to "take them back"?

The book of Genesis tells the story of a man and woman who have been placed in paradise.* Their every need, wish, and whim is available to them. God has placed complete trust in them. They are told to enjoy all the fruits of the garden save two. These two are forbidden. The story continues. A serpent tempts the woman. She yields to the temptation and eats of the fruit. She convinces the man to do so as well. When they hear God walking in the garden they feel guilty. They know they have done wrong. They run and hide from God, but God finds them.

God confronts the man. "Did you do that which you were not supposed to do?" The man's answer is classic and goes right to the heart of what it is to be a human. "This woman that you gave me made me do it." The man tries to avoid taking responsibility. He finds a scapegoat. The woman follows suit. "The serpent made me do it."

If the person who has hurt us begs our forgiveness while at the same time engaging in denial then clearly their repentance is not real. If their energy is put into rationalizing their behavior, trying to justify what they have done, making excuses or looking for a scapegoat, we have reason to be cautious before reconciling with them. Healing is found in **repentance**. The four aspects of repentance are **responsibility, contrition, confession, and resolution.** Forgiveness becomes possible when we hear them accept **responsibility**. Obviously, we recognize that all of us are vulnerable to temptation. None of us are omniscient. We

---

* Genesis 2

have all made mistakes. We have all sinned in thought, word, deed, or omission. The reason that they put erasers on the end of pencils is because people make mistakes. The reason that we have a delete key on our computers is because people are not perfect.

WE NEED TO HEAR THE PERSON WHO HURT US TAKE RESPONSIBILITY FOR THEIR BEHAVIOR.

To say this does not mean that we shrug our shoulders in the face of wrong. It does not mean that we wink and look the other direction. There can be no cheap grace. There can be no justification or rationalization. Even if everybody is doing something that does not make "it" right. Even if nobody is doing it that does not make it wrong. We take responsibility for the pain we have inflicted on another. In taking responsibility, we begin the healing process. We need to hear the person who hurt us take responsibility for their behavior. We need to hear them say with every penitent "through my own fault, through my own fault, through my own grievous fault."

The second phase of the healing process is **contrition.** We need to know that they have come to terms with the pain that they have inflicted. We want to know that if they could go back in time and undo what they have done, they would. If they could erase it from history they would. We need to know that they are contrite not because they have been caught. They are contrite not because they want to get rid of the feelings of guilt. They are contrite because they were wrong and they have hurt another. The ability to feel empathy for us is a major portion of contrition.

We need to know that the person who has hurt us recognizes the pain that they have brought into our life. We need to know that they are not dismissive of our suffering, but that through their tears they are suffering with us. It is when the tormentor identifies with the tormented that the pain is shared and our own load is lifted.

Confession is the third aspect that can bring healing. We confess to God those sins that we have committed against God. We must confess to the persons we have injured the sins we have committed against them. We often think that we can live with our secrets. **We fail to realize that we don't keep secrets. Our secrets keep us!** Like termites, the secrets we keep eat away at our lives. They eat away at our relationships. More often than not, our sins are not secret. Those who know us and love us are well aware of what we have done or not done. They have already sensed our distance. They intuitively know we have changed. We are more transparent than we might want to believe. What those who care about us don't always know is whether or not we are sorry. They don't know whether or not we intend to repeat the behavior if we think we can get by with it. We do not keep secrets. Our secrets keep us. Ultimately, they will destroy us, and the very relationships we are trying to protect.

Adam and Eve in the Genesis story only needed to say to God, "Yes, we did it and we are so sorry." Healing is found in those words. Forgiveness becomes possible when those healing words of confession are uttered. Not only do those we have hurt need to hear us say these words, but we need to hear ourselves say them. These words are prescriptive. They are essential to the healing process.

When the other asks us to forgive them, reconciliation becomes an alternative. If the one who has hurt us continues in their rationalizations, if their tears are but tears for themselves because they got caught, then reconciliation is not an alternative. If their confession is uttered out of fear for themselves and not because they have come to terms with the harm they have inflicted, caution is still advised. If, on the other hand, the confession is combined with healthy quantities of responsibility and contrition, the doors to reconciliation are more easily opened. We need to hear them honestly and contritely ask us to forgive them.

The fourth phase of the healing process is equally critical. The fourth phase involves **learning and changing**. In the fourth phase, we need to know that the person who hurt us has learned from their ways. We want to hear them acknowledge the insights they have gained about themselves through this behavior. What did this mistake teach them? How are they going to be different? How is their life going to be different? How are they going to handle similar temptations in a different fashion? How are their lives going to be better in the future? What are they going to do to try to help those they have injured find healing? Do they need to make restitution? How will this pain that they have inflicted help them grow and mature? We may need them to answer all of these questions and others for us. They are a critical part of the healing process. Such a discussion will not be easy. But then again, we have already acknowledged that forgiving is not easy.

I love the prayer that has been attributed to an old black slave. "Lord, I know that I am not all I am supposed to be. Lord, I know that I am not yet what I am gonna be. But Lord, I sure thank you that I'm not what I used to be." This is a prayer that makes reconciliation a real possibility.

"RECONCILIATION MAY NOT ALWAYS BE PERFECT"

Reconciliation with the person who has injured us helps make forgiveness real. Reconciliation, however, must not be confused with restoration. Restoration means that we restore the person to their former place in our lives as though the betrayal never occurred. Restoration will be discussed more fully in

Chapter Six. Reconciliation, on the other hand, may not be perfect. It may not put things back just the way they were before the breech in your relationship. The offense may change the nature of your relationship forever. Reconciliation may bring closure to the past and to the hurt. It may require you to redefine your relationship. It may be a new relationship or a different kind of relationship. Reconciliation helps the hurting to stop and it helps you leave the past in the past.

Let me share with you three different scenarios of spousal betrayal in heterosexual marriage. While the cases are true, I have amended the names and some circumstances for purposes of confidentiality. In each case there has been reconciliation, but each reconciliation is different. None are perfect.

A man we will call Alex had been happily married for fourteen years. He and his wife had two children, ages ten and twelve. He was a successful businessman in his own right, but he was also supported by a healthy trust fund. His wife had been a homemaker, church and community volunteer for the greater portion of their marriage. As the children grew older, she wanted to go back to the university and acquire a Master's Degree in her area of interest. The university was about thirty miles from their home. A few months into her studies, Alex became suspicious when she began to return later and later in the evenings from her classes. She began to contrive excuses to spend the night at the university to work late on projects in the library or for early classes the next morning.

Alex became suspicious. He employed a private detective. The photographs confirmed his suspicions, but Alex wanted to see it for himself. He went with the detective one evening only to witness his wife snuggling up to a student fifteen years her junior in a local coffee house. They followed them to a motel where she and the student checked in. He and the detective confronted them as they left the motel the next morning. His wife begged his forgiveness. She wanted them to go into marriage counseling. She had been unhappy for years.

Alex attempted the marriage counseling with her, but as he put it, "I simply could not turn off the tape. It would play over and over in my mind. I could not get the image of her going to him out of my mind. The very thought of her lying to me in order to go have sex with him was just too much for me. I spent my days walking around with the sensation of wanting to vomit. I would wake up in the middle of the night in sweats, sick to my stomach, with the tape running in living color. I got to where I could not stand to look at her. I could not have sex with her. I found her disgusting. She was dirty and not trustworthy. In fact, I no longer found her worthy of my love."

While his wife could not deny the evidence when confronted with the video tape, she refused to accept responsibility for her choice. She blamed Alex for her betrayal of her marriage vows. He had not been a good husband, she had been angry with him for years, he was stingy with the money, he did not pay her enough attention and the litany went on. Alex's wife never displayed any aspect of the repentance process beyond tears and appeals to not divorce her for the sake of the children. Even with marital therapy, reconciliation was not a healthy option for Alex.

Alex divorced his wife. He did forgive her. They continue to this day to have an amicable relationship for the sake of the children. His ex-wife has been married and divorced twice since her marriage to Alex. In this particular case, Alex simply could not reconcile with his wife, and continued an amicable relationship with her. He did not however, restore her to the marriage.

The second case is similar, but only this time the roles are reversed. This time it is the wife who has been betrayed. Through their twenty-some years of marriage, she had suspected her husband Bruce of philandering on many occasions. His hunting clothes from the trips with the guys had too often smelled of perfume. She too employed the assistance of a private detective. What she learned shocked her. Her husband had been engaging in a long-term affair with the same woman for several years.

When she confronted him, he too, wanted forgiveness. He was willing to go to counseling. They went to counseling and she reconciled with him. They continued to see the counselor periodically, and the marriage appeared to be secure. In some ways, she thought their relationship was better than ever. Then one afternoon she received a telephone call from a man who refused to identify himself. He simply told her to get into her car and drive to an apartment address in the next city twenty miles away. She needed to go now. "Be prepared," the voice told her. "Your husband is up to his old tricks again." She did as the man suggested and she discovered exactly what she had been told.

Of course, she was devastated. Her husband had never broken off the relationship with the other woman. Once again, there were the tears of remorse. There were the promises and the appeals to go to counseling. He wanted to renew their marriage vows in the church. Since they did not live in a community property state, he would put half of everything he owned in her name. She could have anything she wanted. He would do whatever was required. Then Bruce told on himself one day during a counseling session, He shouted at his wife, "What will people think? I can't have my mother know what kind of person I have been. It would kill her. Besides, if you divorce me I will lose my job; my reputation in this community will be ruined. We have to stay married."

Even in light of this confession the woman found that she simply could not bring herself to divorce him, but she was not sure just how to stay married to him. "I don't love him like I used to. I used to think he was the most wonderful man in the world. I trusted him completely. I always knew he was somewhat of a flirt. When I would get jealous and say something to him, he would tell me he was just being friendly. We would fight about his flirtations some, but I never thought he would do anything like this. Now, I wonder just how many others there have been. I have decided to stay married to him, but I will never again feel the same way about him. The innocence we once shared is gone. The freshness I felt for him is now stale. I can't stop myself from wondering whether or not he is thinking about her and calling her on the telephone. I will never again be able to trust him like I did before. Our lovemaking is now routine. I have to force myself. I simply cannot give myself to him like I used too. He has destroyed all the good things I felt about him. "

They did stay married. The wife agreed to keep up the pretense. Even though none of the four steps of repentance were evident, the marriage continues. As for Bruce, he is up to his old tricks.

The third case of betrayal came as a complete surprise to John, but it should not have surprised him. The evidence was always there. He had just chosen to ignore it. He and his wife of twelve years were taking the children to their lake house for the weekend. His wife left early to prepare the house. He and the children would come later in the day. John stopped for gasoline at a truck stop just a few miles from the lake house. He went into the adjoining cafe to pay for his gasoline. Snuggled up in the booth were his wife and another man. John could see from his viewpoint that the man had his hand underneath her skirt. She was whispering in his ear and laughing. John turned and ran into the bathroom.

John did not confront his wife at that time. In fact, they had their weekend at the cabin, but he began to watch her with new eyes. They had dinner with their neighbors at the lake.

The neighbors had another couple with them for the weekend as houseguests. John took notice how his wife took a special interest in the visiting husband. She managed to sit next to the man and not John at the dinner table. He began to recall how she often would go sit next to another man at dinner tables in the interest of "getting to know them better." If he said anything to her about it on the way home, she would get angry and accuse him of petty jealousy. He also began to recall how she did not stay with him at parties, but often would disappear for the entire evening and then blame him for "losing her." His antenna were now up. He caught her whispering something in the man's ear. He noticed that soon after, the man had both of his hands under the table. At one point in the afternoon, John noticed that both his wife and the man were missing. He found them in the backyard away from the house. Supposedly they were "just talking." John too, employed a private detective.

His discovery made him ill. He discovered that his wife was an unbelievable flirt and that several of her relationships had in fact been sexual. The detective began to do some selective interviews around the community. John was shocked to discover the number of men who were willing to acknowledge, and even boast to the detective, that his wife had "come on" to them. In more than one instance they bragged about having sex with her. One of the men even had pictures that he turned over to the detective. He gave the detective pictures that he had taken without her knowledge, but had shown to other men in the community.

When John confronted his wife, she too begged forgiveness. She wanted to go to counseling. She just had not known how to tell John how mad she was at him. She did not know how to get him to pay more attention to her. She would never do it again. They did go to counseling. She answered every question he asked her about her past relationships. John believed that she was truthful with him. She took complete responsibility for her behavior. She did not try to blame John or put up any kind of smoke screen. Through her tears John saw just how wounded she was. He believed that she hurt for him as well. John forgave his wife and reconciled with her.

They have a new and different kind of marriage. John told me that in many ways it was a better marriage, but like Alex, in the first case, John still wrestles with the memories. When he least expects it, the memory of his wife snuggled up with the man in the truck stop would come to mind. The pictures that another man took of his wife having sex with him continue to haunt John. He still has a difficult time trusting his wife not to hurt him again. While he believes her contrition is real and he has no reason to believe that she was being unfaithful to him, he does not find her as desirable and attractive as he once did. He had thought she was a lady. Now, that image of her is completely gone.

For the sake of the children, he decided to tough it out with her. They even managed to have some good times together. "It just isn't the same. I used to love her with every fiber of my being. I thought I was the luckiest man in the world. Now, I just feel like a fool. I remember so many times now that I had suspicions about her, but I chose to trust her. I can't help but wonder just how many men there are out there laughing at me. It is so humiliating."

The marriage manuals give a variety of reasons for a marriage partner choosing to commit adultery. They vary from the thrill and variety of the sex to the genuine need for intimacy. Regardless of the reason, adultery destroys the trust. The betrayed partner will feel physically and emotionally abused. Reconciliation is possible. I know many couples that have been able to put things back together and move forward. On the other hand, I also know that even in the best scenarios, the marriage for the offended party never again has the innocence and luster that it did before.

In the three cases I described for you, one ended in divorce and two decided to continue their marriage. In each case, the couples made the commitment to forgive and to try to move forward with their lives. Far too many couples choose to nurture their hurt, anger and bitterness toward one another. Too many couples end up trying to use the children, if there are any, as weapons to beat each other up. Too often, the offended party decides to take the moral high ground and use the act of infidelity as a Damocles Sword. It will hang over the other's head and they will drop it on them when they least expect it.

FORGIVENESS CANNOT TAKE PLACE
IF THE PAIN IS NURTURED.

Whether the couple decides to stay married or divorce, renew their life commitment or separate, forgiveness is required. The past needs to be left in the past. The hurt and the pain will haunt the relationship for years even when forgiveness is granted. Forgiveness cannot take place if the pain is nurtured. We must forgive the partner who has betrayed us. We need to do it for ourselves. We need to do it for our children if we have them. We need to do it whether they ask our forgiveness or not. Forgiving a partner an act of sexual betrayal is not easy. It may be one of the toughest wounds ever to tear at a couple's relationship.

Reconciliation is a real alternative even in the face of infidelity. If we attempt it simply utilizing our own resources, we will find the effort exhausting and disappointing. However, if we approach reconciliation utilizing the spiritual resources available to us, we will discover that God is still working miracles. The Almighty can even work a miracle in our life. Reconciliation is always a choice for us, but it requires that those who have offended us be truly repentant.

Questions for Reflection and/or Action

1. If you have been hurt by another what particular words and actions do you need to hear them say and do to know that they are truly repentant in each of the following areas?

    A. They have accepted responsibility?

    B. They are truly sorry for their actions?

    C. Their confession and request for forgiveness is genuine?

    D. They are changing their lives so that they will not do it again?

    E. They have learned a lesson from the experience and are trying to be a better person?

Step Five Alternative

"When Reconciliation is Not a Choice"

Some people will never take responsibility for their action. Some will never come to terms with the pain they have caused. Some will rationalize their acts of sin and evil as righteous and justified. We cannot reconcile with them, but for our soul's sake we still must forgive them.

We have already allowed for the fact that there will be times in our lives when we will need to forgive another person, but reconciliation with that person may not be desirable or even advisable. If there has been a pattern of verbal, emotional, and/ or physical abuse, reconciliation may not be warranted. For our own soul's health, we will certainly want to and need to forgive the person. However, to return that person to their former station in our life simply may not be wise. We must forgive, but reconciliation is not always possible. Reconciliation may not be desirable. Reconciliation, in some instances, may not even be advisable.

There are situations in which the offense has been criminal in nature. In such cases, reconciliation may not be an option.

When the offender has not repented of their deed, reconciliation is not possible. Sometimes, we discover that there has been a pattern of betrayal throughout our marriage or relationship with the person. The discovery of this pattern is so heart-wrenching that reconciliation is simply not an option.

> **WE MAY BE SO HURT OR SO BURNED-OUT WE SIMPLY CANNOT BRING OURSELVES TO RECONCILE.**

Once the bloom has been removed from the stem, it cannot be put back on again. When the crystal glass has been smashed, it cannot be repaired. The relationship simply cannot be put back together. Even when reconciliation is desirable, the relationship will never again be the same. Once innocence and trust have been destroyed, they cannot be recreated. There can be a new relationship. There can be a different kind of relationship, but we cannot regain the freshness and purity that were there before. Eden can be desired, but Eden cannot be recreated.

I am reminded of a woman who came to see me after discovering that her husband had been in an adulterous relationship. Through her tears she told me of his pleas to be forgiven. He confessed his undying love and his complete contrition. He would do anything in order to rebuild their marriage. I asked the woman if she still loved her husband. She sobbed that she did love him but not like she used to. I suggested that this might be good. Perhaps she could discover a new love for him. Perhaps they could have a different kind of love, an even better love.

If we have had an employee or business associate who has been stealing from us, we need to forgive them, but we may not want to give them the combination to the safe again. If we have a child who has been rebellious, uncontrollable, and acting out chemically or violently, we will want to forgive them, but tough love may be called for before restoring them to the family home. If we have had an unfaithful spouse, again, we will want to forgive them, but sharing our marriage bed with them again may not be advisable.

"WHEN WE DON'T HAVE THE STRENGTH TO RECONCILE"

In some cases reconciliation may be advisable. It may even be desirable, but we simply do not have the emotional resources to achieve it. We may be so hurt or so burned out we simply cannot bring ourselves to reconcile. This may be because the offense has triggered other painful memories for us and the hurt has become even more gangrenous. Consider the person who has previously reconciled with an unfaithful spouse only to have their trust betrayed again. Their emotional glass just may be too shattered to subject themselves to the possibility of yet another betrayal.

I remember interviewing a candidate for employment. One of the routine interview questions I ask is this: "What do you do when you make a mistake?" This particular interview candidate astounded me by responding, "I don't make mistakes!" It is important for us to keep in mind that the opposite of holiness is not sin. The opposite of holiness is self-righteousness. Again, the scriptures remind us, "All have sinned. All have come short of the glory of God."* In the real world, however, we have to recognize that there are those people who can and will hurt us, but will never show any remorse for what they have done. In fact, given the opportunity, they would hurt us again. Spiritual teachings acknowledge that there are "children of the light and children of darkness.*

* Romans 3:23

71

Scripture describes Jesus spending forty days in the wilderness being tempted by the Prince of Darkness. The enlightening moment for contemporary Christians is the realization that Satan quoted scriptures in order to justify deeds of evil.

Most priests' manuals contain rites of exorcism. Yet, in spite of all these ancient and contemporary teachings on the reality of evil, the larger Church appears reluctant to face it. Instead of naming evil as evil, we often resort to "psycho-babble" to rationalize away hurtful behaviors. We too often dismiss a person displaying evil tendencies with the label "anti-social behavior." Or we label them as compulsive, a control freak, or an angry person. They are simply projecting their own insecurities, guilt, fear, etc. onto another.

Scott Peck in his book "People of the Lie" tries to get us to come to terms with the reality of evil. Karl Menninger in an earlier publication attempted much of the same. His book was entitled, "Whatever Happened to Sin?" The common theme in both books is that we must resist the temptation to rationalize, justify, and overly analyze hurtful behavior. Sometimes, evil needs to be acknowledged and dealt with accordingly. The thing that I find most fascinating about these two popular works on evil is that they were done by psychiatrists and not by theologians.

People of Faith are naturally hesitant to name evil. The foundation of faith is a God of love. We want to believe that there is hope for every person. We are slow to acknowledge the reality that some folks intentionally and willfully seek the destruction of others. Sometimes these acts of evil are motivated by simple envy. There are individuals who have little or no development of the superego. Still others have deluded themselves into believing that the pain they cause is for some greater good. They do not see their hurtful actions as evil at all.

Each time I have come face to face with evil, I have had to come to terms with the clever ways that wolves can clothe themselves in sheep's clothing. I have been amazed at the number of times I have witnessed acts of mean-spiritedness, betrayal, hurt and cruelty justified with quotations from Holy Scripture. We Christians need to be continually reminded that Satan quoted scripture in order to tempt Jesus. Then again, it is particularly revealing when intelligent, well-educated people cannot see the darkness in their own deeds. It is important for us to remember that the classic definition for evil is the complete absence of empathy. The Reverend Billy Graham, speaking at a memorial service for the victims of the Oklahoma City bombing, defined evil as "what we are capable of doing when our lives are without God."

"WOLVES IN SHEEP CLOTHING"

There is a phenomenon in the religious community today that has received the clinical name "Clergy Killers". It has reached epidemic proportions in the church and synagogues. Members of the clergy and their families become the victims of threats, intimidation, and trauma. They are abused by the very people they are attempting to serve. The goal of the clergy killers is to remove them from office and if possible destroy their ministries. There is a proliferation of books, articles, and research projects on this evil. Some estimate that hundreds of clergy and their families experience this trauma every year. The point I want to make is that even within the religious community there are those that do terrible things to the shepherd who serves them, but have no qualms of conscience. No regrets. No remorse, but to the contrary, justify their deeds as being righteous.

To this day, this phenomenon continues to bring incredible grief to clergy and their families. The wounds left by these clergy killers on the other members of the congregation last for decades. Congregations are left divided by their handiwork. People who used to be close friends no longer speak to one another. Formerly active members of the church find themselves unable to return to worship.

Those who target clergy for destruction mirror the profile of many in our world who do not see their deeds as evil. They appear to be totally unable to comprehend the pain that their actions bring into the lives of those around them. They are oblivious to the destruction they have brought into the lives of those around them. With the taste of blood in their mouths, the crown of victory on their heads, and their adrenaline pumping, they celebrate their victories. They have "saved the parish, the synagogue, the museum, symphony, neighborhood, family…" They have done the right thing. They did what needed to be done. They did what no one else had the courage to do. They continue on as parish leaders, even serving in elected offices, as though nothing ever happened. When confronted, their supporters will respond along with them that everyone owes them a debt of gratitude.

Those who are oblivious to the pain they cause others have some other observable characteristics as well. They live with the illusion of their own perfection. They deny responsibility for their own behavior. Their favorite defense mechanisms are projection and scapegoating. These folks have perfected to a fine art form the ability to project onto others those things they find most unacceptable in themselves.

This points to yet other factors that are descriptive of this profile. They are consumed with their public image. They put their energies into maintaining an image of social superiority. They are more concerned with what "their social group" thinks of them than what God thinks. Hence, their passion to tear down others in an effort to make themselves appear larger. Obviously, with such people there will never be any repentance. Without repentance there can be no reconciliation.

"We Are All Imperfect"

Archbishop William Temple is credited with stating "the Church is not a haven for the saints, but a hospital for sinners." Yet surveys of the majority of the members of the Church feel that they are without sin. They have not done anything wrong. When compared with others, they are not as bad as other folks are. And, they are quite happy to name these other sinners for you. The question begs an answer for many of us. Is the church a recovery hospital for sinners suffering the consequences of their sins? Or, is the church a monument for the pretense of our own goodness? I cannot help but think about just how grievous it is to merge the words "self" and "righteous" into one.

The Bible reminds us "if we walk in the light as God is light, we cannot be content with any darkness within us."* As the saints grew in holiness, they did not become more comfortable with themselves. They did not elevate themselves over others. Their disciples tell us that they became more discontented with their imperfections. St. Paul lamented, "I do those things that I do not want to do and I leave undone those things I want to do."*

Several years ago, the popular phrase in society was, "I'm O.K. You're O.K." While that is a nice "feel-good phrase," it is important for us to remember that it is not the Christian gospel. The gospel of Christ is not "I'm O.K. You're O.K." It is not "I'm O.K., but you're not O.K." Likewise, it is not "I'm not O.K, but you're O.K." The gospel of Jesus Christ is "I'm

---

* Ephesians 5:8
* Romans 7:20

not O.K. You're not O.K., but by the grace of God we are both O.K."

Daily we can strive to be better and do better. Daily we can reach for the standard that eludes us. Daily we can examine our consciences and see clearly the mistakes we have made. And daily we must live with the knowledge that in spite of our best efforts we have not been perfect and the sins that we see and the ones that we do not see convict us. When our super-egos, our consciences, are developed we will feel guilty when we have injured another. In spiritually healthy individuals, guilt is to the soul what pain is to the body. It tells us that something is wrong.

Professor William Muel of Yale Divinity School has stated, "Imperfection is not the corruption of history, it is the essence of history." Our cries for a perfect world blessed by a perfect Church filled with perfect people flies in the face of reality. Spiritually healthy people do not use the universality of sin as a way to justify hurting others. To the contrary spiritually healthy people are convicted of their imperfections. They are aware of their wrongdoing.

Those who take delight in confronting others with their sins often do so from a pretense of moral or spiritual superiority. They pretend to be without sin. They reason that this qualifies them to sit in judgment on the failings of others. **Such pretense of moral superiority will consistently fail to bring anyone to repentance. Only a repentant sinner can help another sinner find healing**.

> ### ONLY A REPENTANT SINNER CAN
> ### HELP ANOTHER SINNER FIND HEALING.

The story is told that while St. Francis of Assisi was dying, he was resting on a cot, without a mattress, made of wood. It is said that he instructed his disciples to take him from the cot and put him on the floor. He whispered, "I am not worthy to meet my Lord in the comfort of a bed."

Contrast St. Francis with evil behavior that is oblivious to the pain it causes others. Contrast the lives of the saints with folks who refuse to admit they have any imperfections. How do we discern those who become more and more satisfied with themselves in their Christian journey? The energy that is put into maintaining an illusion of moral and social perfection is revealing. The scriptures remind us, "If we say that we have no sin, we deceive ourselves and the truth is not in us."* You and I are called to live with a growing discontent for our own imperfections.

I remember hearing the story of the preacher who was called to a parish in a logging community in the Pacific Northwest. The preacher soon learned that some of the members of the congregation were pulling the logs out of the river that were destined for the mill. Other timber companies had cut the logs further up stream. The ends of the logs would be marked with the company insignia. These members of his congregation would cut off the ends of the logs, put their own marks on them, and put them back into the river.

The preacher knew that he was going to have to address this practice. He preached his first sermon and titled it; "Thou shalt not steal!" Nothing changed. He preached his second sermon and titled it, "Thou shalt not covet!" Again, nothing changed. The preacher decided he would have to be more direct. He titled his third sermon, "Thou shalt not cut off the ends of thy neighbors logs." They got the point.

To walk in the light requires us to be just that specific. Before we open our mouths to utter a word, we need to ask, will this word communicate love or hate? Before we lift our

---

* 1 John 1:8

hand to do a single deed, we need to ask, will this deed bring healing or division? Each word and deed requires us to be specific. Will they communicate understanding or prejudice, reconciliation or bitterness, unity or division? Will our words and our works build up or tear down, heal or hurt, give life or bring death?

"FORGIVE EVEN WHEN RECONCILIATION IS NOT POSSIBLE"

We have to come to terms with the evidence that, for whatever reason, we will encounter people who are unable to be this specific. People who will remain oblivious to the pain that they have inflicted on others will hurt us. They will never accept responsibility for their own behavior. Their hurtful words or deeds were caused by an imperfection in us. There is nothing wrong with them. They are without sin. They will blame, justify, project, and scapegoat. They will never apologize to us. They will never ask our forgiveness. They will go to their graves living with the illusion of their own perfection. They will maintain the illusion of social and moral superiority with their dying breath. We will never hear them say, "I am sorry." Still, for our own physical, emotional, and spiritual health we must forgive them. Forgiving them is the only way that we will get our life back.

"Questions for Reflection and/or Action"

1. How would your life be different if you could forgive the person who hurt you even if they never ask your forgiveness?

2. Is the person who has hurt you incapable of taking responsibility? Could they be a person who suffers with a social or psychological disorder?

3. What will your life be like if you continue to wait for an apology that may never come?

4. Do you believe you can forgive the person even if they never apologize? What specific things do you need to do?

5. Can you think of a person who has repented of their sins and now has an effective ministry of healing with other sinners?

STEP SIX

"WHEN RESTORATION IS A CHOICE"

To restore the person who has hurt us to their former place in our lives is to move forward with them as though they never traumatized us. Restoration is the fullest expression of forgiveness. It requires that the one who hurt us not only be sorry for their sin. It requires that they change their ways. They must make restitution. They must become a new creation with the old passing away.

So far I have tried to describe what it means to forgive others for our own mental, physical, and spiritual health. I offered a description of forgiving and reconciling with the commitment to begin again, even though things will never again be as they were before. I have also tried to describe the impact of forgiving others even when reconciliation is not a possibility. Now, we must look at the most difficult part of forgiveness. How can we restore the person to their formal status as though the sin had never occurred?

To understand this part of the forgiveness process, I want to take another look at the most familiar story in the world on forgiveness. The Parable of the Prodigal Son* is often presented as a lesson in forgiveness. It is not. It is a story about restoration. The elder brother who kept all the ordinances and had done as his father wanted him to do would not have objected nearly as much if the issue were simply one of forgiveness. Oh yes, we can certainly understand the importance of forgiving an offender. We need to do that for ourselves. What set the eldest son off was the fact that the father restored the son to his rightful place in the family. Not only was he restored to his position with all of the rights and privileges he had abused, but the father also gave him a party and poured additional honor upon him.

I should like to contend that it is not forgiveness that causes us to break with the teachings of Jesus on reconciliation, it is restoration. Forgiving and forgetting can be very difficult for us, but by God's grace we can learn to exercise them. It is very difficult to take exception with restoring a person spiritually. To restore folks physically to their former rights and privileges takes an extra measure of grace on our part. To not only restore a penitent person, but to pour additional honors on them feels like adding insult to injury. There can be no ring, no robe, and no fatted calf.

In the Church I have often come to the defense of those who have objected to persons serving on the vestry, being a lay reader, serving the chalice, being recommended for ordination, or some other leadership position in the Church because of a past sin. "They are not good enough." Some have said to me that they should not be allowed to have that honor or privilege. They cry, "They are not worthy!" Yet, the God of Love reminds us that none of us are worthy. I once heard that justice could be defined as having all the consequences of our sins fall on us and no one else. None of us want justice. On the Day of Judgment we will all cry for mercy and grace.

---

* Luke 15

"Restoration Completes the Forgiveness Process"

I have been hearing private confessions almost from the day I was ordained to the priesthood. I made my first private confession in seminary. Each time I have granted absolution, I have concluded with these words from the prayer book, "The Lord has put away all your sins."*

> ## Only you and I can make the forgiveness of God real.

I have taught that when a priest pronounces absolution, the penitent is being restored to the full fellowship of the community. I have taught that when the priest says, "God forgives you," they are also saying –

> I forgive you, the Altar Guild forgives you, the choir forgives you, the Men's group forgives you; the acolytes forgive you, the Women of the Church forgives you, the diocese forgives you, the National Church forgives you, the entire Anglican Communion forgives you, and the Church Catholic on earth and in Heaven forgives you. Now go, sin no more. You are fully restored to the body. You are completely reconciled to God and to the people in God's Church.

I have taught further that we in the Church should treat one another as though we had just stepped out of the confessional. Who knows? We might have just done that very thing. Clearly, Jesus has given to His Church the power to forgive sins. "If you forgive the sins of any they are forgiven. If you retain the sins of any they are retained."* This power

* John 20:22
* Book of Common Prayer, page 448.

does not, however, manifest itself only in the reciting of the words of absolution. Forgiveness has to be manifested in people's lives. Only you and I can make the forgiveness of God real. If you and I don't treat one another in a forgiving manner, then forgiveness remains only an ideology.

Can you imagine the healing that was made possible in the early Church services of reconciliation? Imagine a group of Christians seated in a circle. The bishop or priest stands. "My brothers and sisters in Christ Jesus, I want to confess to you that I have sinned in the following ways." The cleric then publicly lists his specific sins in thought, word, deed, and omission. Then the cleric concludes, "For these and all my sins I ask your forgiveness." Then one by one all around the circle the members stand and make their confessions.

When all have concluded the cleric again stands and announces, "Our Lord Jesus Christ told his disciples that if we would confess our sins one to another that God would be faithful and just to forgive us our sins and cleanse us from all unrighteousness. In the name of Jesus of Nazareth I declare that our sins have been buried with him in his death so that we can live anew in his resurrection."

Can you imagine the healing, the reconciliation, and the restoration of relationships made possible in such a service? I once heard a Bishop say that sooner or later we will all confess our sins to another person. Some will boast about their accomplishments to another under a cloud of darkness. In that case, no absolution is wanted or desired. Some will pay a psychiatrist or counselor several hundred dollars per hour to let them unload their deceit. Most of us simply need to confess to a priest or spiritual director who can then assure us that we are forgiven.

I am an Episcopalian. I love the Episcopal Church. Most days I can't figure out why everyone doesn't want to be an

Episcopalian. But so much for my tunnel vision on denominationalism. The thing that makes the Episcopal Church so important to me is that I perceive the vast majority of Episcopalians to be a people who try to make forgiveness, reconciliation, and restoration real. I have stated emphatically that the Episcopal Church is the Church for those people who do not feel they are good enough to belong to any other church. Of course, I know that the Episcopal Church falls short of my ideal in this area. But I can't help but think that such is closer to the vision of the Church held up for us in the scriptures.

Forgiveness, without restoration, is just as incomplete as is forgiveness without true repentance. If a person has truly repented of their sin and amended their life to follow again the commandments of God, then the words of absolution will be as a noisy gong or clanging cymbal if they are not followed with restoration. Restoration makes the forgiveness real. The intent of the Christian Sacrament of Reconciliation has always been full restoration. "Those who, because of notorious sins, had been separated from the body of the faithful were reconciled by penitence and forgiveness, and restored to the fellowship of the Church."*

RESTORATION MAKES FORGIVENESS REAL.

What kind of ending would it have been if the Father had only forgiven the prodigal son? "Yes, I can see that your repentance is real so I forgive you, but you are going to have to sleep in the servant's quarters. You have already blown your inheritance, so don't expect to receive anything else from me. You are forgiven, but I will never let you forget what you have done. You are forgiven, but you have forfeited all your rights and privileges as a member of this family.

---

* Book of Common Prayer, page 265.

"RESTORATION REQUIRES A CELEBRATION"

Thank God that is not the way Jesus ended this parable. "Bring out a robe – the best one – and put it on him; put a ring on his finger and sandals on his feet. And get the fatted calf and kill it, and let us eat and celebrate, for this son of mine was dead and is alive again; he was lost and is found. And they began to celebrate."*

The eldest son would have held his righteous superiority over the prodigal son. Jesus did not allow that to happen in the parable. You and I must not allow that to happen to one another. If the repentance of the person who has sinned against us is real, the challenge is to not only forgive and to reconcile, but also to restore. If they are making amendments in their lives in such a way that they will strive not to fall to temptation again, can we not risk restoring them to their former place in our lives? If they are striving to learn from their mistakes and make positive steps toward overcoming their weakness, will restoration not complete the cycle of forgiveness for us?

Hear this scenario. Jim and Becky made an appointment to see me. Becky told me that she had confessed to Jim that she had been unfaithful to him. She became too friendly with a co-worker and one thing led to another. Obviously, Jim was devastated. Becky cried through most of the interview. Her contrition was so real. They had been going to a therapist. She was learning how to express her needs and not to expect Jim to read her mind. Jim was learning not to put his career first and take a little extra effort to compliment Becky and tell her how pretty she was. They both were learning the need to spend more time with each other without their children. They both had learned so much about themselves, each other, and nurturing a loving relationship. Jim was not ready to say that Becky's

---

* Luke 15:23

affair was the best thing that had ever happened to them and he wished that it had never happened, but it was a wake-up call for both of them. They now wanted me to help them strengthen their spiritual life together.

We talked about the importance of regular worship together. Holding hands in worship and kneeling together to receive communion would become a priority for them. We discussed the importance of sharing their faith in God with one another. We made a plan that for them that included praying together, sharing a ministry of visiting the elderly together, and participating in an annual marriage renewal weekend.

We also read the marriage service and agreed that weekly they would read the prayers in the Book of Common Prayer appointed for a wedding. They would continue to take special note of the intercession, "Give them grace when they hurt each other to seek one another's forgiveness and yours."*

Then we talked about the importance of transforming their lovemaking into a spiritual experience. I emphasized the importance of words of affection, the importance looking in one another's eyes, the importance of focusing on one another, and of taking their time for endearments both before and after their love-sharing.

A few months after that interview, Jim and Becky moved to another city. They felt it important that Becky get completely away from her co-worker who continued to pursue her. I hear from them each Christmas. There is always a wonderful picture of the entire family, but they always include yet another picture. They include an updated romantic portrait of just the two of them. Along with their pictures they also include a bottle of my favorite wine. They sign their card, "Just Like a Fine Wine, Love – Jim and Becky".

---

* Book of Common Prayer, Page 429.

Forgiving those who have hurt us even when they beg our forgiveness is not easy. Forgiving those who seem oblivious to the pain they have caused us is even more difficult. Restoring those who have betrayed us to their previous position in our lives is the most difficult act of grace of all. Forgiveness is a spiritual process. For our own sake, for the sake of those we love, for the sake of those we live and work with on a daily basis – forgiveness is not just the best option. It is the right option. When we consider all that the Almighty has forgiven each one of us, can we really consider doing less for the truly repentant?

Questions for Reflection and/or Action

1. What must the person who has hurt you do before you can restore them to their former position?

2. Do you genuinely want to continue your life with the other person fully in it?

3. How would you like to celebrate your new life together? What would that celebration look like?

4. Why not plan that celebration now?

STEP SEVEN

"NURTURE A FORGIVING HEART"

The pain in life can transform some people into hard, bitter people. Their hearts and their souls become calloused. Others allow the suffering in life to make them even more loving, understanding, forgiving, and accepting of the humanity of others. It is a choice. We all will choose. It doesn't just happen. We choose how we are going to respond.

Some of the most loving, compassionate people I know have suffered unbelievable humiliation, degradation, and hurt in their lives. By the same token, I have known others who have experienced similar or identical trauma react to their hurts by becoming personalities filled with bitterness and resentment. Clearly, some integrate their pain into their spiritual journeys. Their wounds become developmental. They become wounded healers who serve as an inspiration for all those around them. Others continue to pick at their wounds, refusing to let them heal.

It was Anglican author Dorothy Sayer who made the point that there are two types of martyrs. If the pain we experience in life makes us bitter; if we allow pain to harden our hearts and destroy our souls then we become martyrs for the devil. However, if we use the traumas in life to make us more loving, forgiving, and compassionate then we become martyrs for God.

I found the newspaper account of the story to be very moving. I never forgot it. I kept the clipping for years. It all happened one cool November evening in New Iberia, Louisiana. Eighteen-year-old Loretta Bourque and her fiancé David Le Blanc parked on Lover's Lane. That night, Elmo Patrick Sonnier and his brother Eddie forced the young couple from their car at gunpoint. They then drove them to a field twenty miles away. There they handcuffed Le Blanc to a tree. The two brothers then raped his fiancé. They shot each of the teenagers in the back of the head three times with a twenty-two rifle.

Under Louisiana law, when you willfully take the life of another, you have made the decision to forfeit your own. It took several years, but the day did arrive when Elmo Patrick Sonnier was strapped in the electric chair in the Louisiana Department of Corrections. One of those allowed to witness Sonnier's execution was the father of the young girl.

After being strapped into the electric chair, Elmo Patrick Sonnier made the following statement: "I ask God's forgiveness for my sins. I ask the forgiveness of everyone I have ever hurt." Then he looked at the father of the young woman he had raped and murdered. "And, I ask your forgiveness."

The newspaper reported that at this point, Mr. Bourque looked at the man who had committed unbelievable atrocities on his daughter and then brought her short life of promise to an end. Mr. Bourque looked at the man about to meet his Maker and nodded affirmatively, "I forgive you." At 1:15 a.m. that morning, Elmo Patrick Sonnier was pronounced dead.

Now I don't know if Mr. Bourque is a Christian. The newspaper account did not report his religion. I don't even know if he is a religious person. One thing I know for sure, however, is that Mr. Bourque is a man convicted of his own sins. You see, before he could forgive Elmo Patrick Sonnier for the atrocities he committed on his daughter, he had to develop a forgiving heart. A forgiving heart is the natural, or should we say, the supernatural consequence of experiencing forgiveness for oneself.

The above story certainly emphasizes the reality that forgiving is not easy. It may be the most difficult spiritual work we ever do. Forgiving is a choice. We can choose to develop a destructive heart or we can choose to nurture a forgiving heart. We can choose to nurture our anger, resentments, and revenge. We can choose to be frozen in the past, destined to relive old hatreds with our dying breath. We can rehearse our pain until it bitterly oozes out of every pore. In the process, we can destroy ourselves and we may destroy everyone around us. Mr. Bourque, like so many others, chose to forgive and get his life back.

"Letting Pain Make Us More Forgiving"

People who have the greatest difficulty in life trusting other people are the very folks who have not come to terms with their own sins. People who have the greatest difficulty making commitments and giving and receiving love are blind to their own imperfections. The folks who are most critical of others, the ones who are most judgmental, are the very people who have not accepted the disease that is part and parcel of our humanity.

On the other hand, the most forgiving individuals are those who know the power of forgiveness for themselves. The most understanding, the most loving, the most accepting people in the world have experienced the grace of the Almighty. They are in fact called "grace filled." Isn't that a descriptive word?

The biggest surprise in life is not that people sin. The miracle is that people learn to forgive. Those who honestly wrestle with their own dark side are not shocked to discover that their neighbor has given into selfishness, greed, lust, hate, or envy. They are not shocked by those who insist on perpetuating a grudge or nurturing their anger. They are not shocked by those who habitually gossip, criticize, or sit in judgment over others. Those who are aware of their own dark sides are well aware of the reality of evil. The great and wonderful surprise is that we can be forgiven. The really good news is that we can also learn to forgive.

"TURNING GARBAGE INTO GOLD"

Through the power of God, judgmentalism can be turned into understanding. Alienation can be replaced with reconciliation. Selfishness can be transformed into generosity. Resentment can be healed. I believe it was The Reverend Robert Shuller that I first heard use the phrase "God can turn the garbage of our lives into gold."

SIN IS NOT A CRIME TO BE PUNISHED, BUT A DISEASE TO BE HEALED.

Just look at what God has done in the lives of our Biblical heroes. Noah, the chosen survivor of the flood, was a drunk. Moses, the lawgiver, was a murderer. Isaac, the favored son, was a manipulator. Joseph, the interpreter of dreams, was a spoiled brat. David, the King of Israel, was an adulterer and a murderer. Solomon, filled with wisdom, was a materialist. Mary Magdalene, one of the first witnesses of the resurrection, was a prostitute. Peter, the first bishop of the Church, denied Christ three times. Saul, who was responsible for the first Christian martyr, became St. Paul the Apostle.

God always uses imperfect people because there is no other kind. The surprise is not that people sin or make mistakes; the great and wonderful surprise is that God forgives us. The spiritual insight is that God can give you and me the power to forgive each other. The miracle is that God can turn the garbage of our lives into gold.

The Tiffany Company is well known for their stained glass windows. When they constructed their windows, there were always broken pieces of glass left over. Some were chipped. Others were rough. They were the rejects. They had no use. Someone happened on the idea of taking the broken pieces of glass and using them to make lampshades. Tiffany lampshades brighten dark rooms with beautiful light all around the world.

That is exactly what God can do with the broken, chipped, rough pieces in our lives. That is what God can do with those mistakes and moments in our lives that just don't fit into the beautiful picture we would like to paint for ourselves. God can take the rough moments of guilt and shame, redeem them, and turn them into beautiful lights for the entire world to see.

"Sending A Message of Forgiveness"

A few years ago, there was a particular teenage girl that had been very active in her local Methodist Church. She was a leader in the youth program. She volunteered in the nursery and served in the summer Bible School for children. She also had a boyfriend. They were very much in love. One evening their passions got the best of them. They did what they should not have done. The girl became pregnant. Her own religious belief was that she could not get an abortion. She was going to carry the baby to term. She was going to keep the baby. She and the young man would get married. However, she dropped out of church.

Her pastor went to see her and tried to get her to come back to church. She protested. "No one will understand. The church people will just judge me. They will criticize me and gossip about me."

Some of the ladies in the church decided that they wanted to give the girl a baby shower. As you can imagine, other people in the church objected. They worried that a baby shower would be sending the wrong message to the other teenagers. The first group persevered. They were certain about the message they wanted to send the teenagers. They gave the girl the baby shower. They wanted all the teenagers to hear the right message. "God did not send His son into the world to condemn the world, but that through Him, the world might be redeemed."*

There is the power of forgiveness. There is forgiveness at work. When we forgive, we bring healing to ourselves and all those around us. When we forgive, we transform lives. When we forgive, we are able to begin again. When we forgive, our garbage is turned into gold. Forgiving those who have hurt us is a spiritual work. It is not easy, but it is the grace and power of God at work within us.

God can take the broken, chipped, rejected moments in our lives and transform them. God can turn us into beautiful lamps to give light to those who live in their own darkness. When we forgive those who hurt us, we make it possible for them to take the broken pieces of their own lives and do the same. Forgiving those who have hurt us is not easy. The choice remains ours.

* John 3:17

"We Choose How to Live With Our Pain"

Do we want to live our lives rehearsing old hurts and resentments? Do we want to breathe division and hate until we can breathe no longer? Or do we want to be agents of healing? Do we want to be set free from the past so that we can claim the promises of the future? Bitterness or healing, hate or love, division or reconciliation; which will be the hallmarks of our lives? To choose to develop forgiving hearts is a spiritual work. Through the grace of God we can learn to forgive others as we seek forgiveness for ourselves. It very well may be the most critical spiritual work we dare to undertake in this life. But when we consider the alternative, do we really have a choice?

Christians routinely pray the Lord's Prayer. "Forgive us our trespasses as we forgive those who trespass against us."* The prayer does not suggest some sort of conditional exchange. Each time I forgive one I get one forgiven. No, the prayer teaches that to experience forgiveness for ourselves, we have to first deal with the reality and consequences of our own sins. We have to deal with them in such a way that we are led to forgive those who sin against us.

A forgiving heart is a heart that has experienced forgiveness. The unforgiving heart is a heart that has never faced up to the hurts it has caused others. An unforgiving heart has never processed the consequences of its own deeds done and left undone. The unforgiving heart is filled with self-righteousness. The unforgiving heart pretends to be without sin. The unforgiving heart piously assumes the role of judge, jury, and executioner over the sins of others. The unforgiving heart would have us believe that it is above sin and has been Divinely appointed to a place of moral superiority.

---

* Matthew 6

97

I remember hearing the story of the time that Carlyle Marney, the controversial Southern Baptist Preacher, was speaking at a Baptist University. Doctor Marney had gained a reputation for being outspoken. He was a maverick who took delight in throwing curve balls at his listeners. The story is that a young man, a student in the university, asked Carlyle Marney: "Do you really believe that God loves us enough to forgive us all our sins?"

It is reported that Dr. Marney leaned over the podium in order to get a better look at his questioner. "How old are you, boy? You can't be more than eighteen." The student proudly reported that he was nineteen. With that, Dr. Marney began, "Nineteen...nineteen, boy, you don't know the first thing about forgiveness. I'll not even discuss it with you. You can't possibly know the first thing about it."

Marney then began to walk about the stage waving his hands in the air. He returned to the podium, "Son, you don't have a clue as to what it feels like to wake up in the middle of the night with indigestion and heartburn from eating what used to be your favorite food. You don't know what it is to have your body refuse to cooperate with your mind. You don't know the first thing about failure and defeat and I'm not talking about losing some damn football game. Boy, you don't know the first thing about having a friend betray you. I mean really betray you. To be so betrayed you are not sure you will ever recover from the heartache."

Just when everyone thought Marney was finished with the young man, he got his second breath and began again. "You don't have any idea what it is to have your spouse lie to you, your children disappoint you, and your friends desert you. Just wait until you work your fingers to the bone and your business still fails. Wait until you find out what it's like to have incompetent people beneath you promoted over you. Come back in fifty years when life has abused, hurt, and disappointed you. Then, then we'll talk about forgiveness."

Once again Marney began to walk around the stage flaying his arms and muttering to himself. Just as the young man was about to sit down, the account is that Marney called his attention one last time. "By then, young man, you will have learned all about forgiveness for yourself. When you have had your dreams shattered. When you have had your ideals slaughtered. When your goals have eluded you, then you'll know about forgiveness. Either you will have developed a forgiving heart by then or you will be a bitter old man. You will be filled with anger and resentment. You will be so self-righteous that no one will want to be around you. Only you won't know it, because no one will have the guts to tell you. They will just stay out of your way as much as possible and you will be so pious that you won't understand why. Either you will be a bitter old man or you will have developed a forgiving heart. If you have developed a forgiving heart you will bring peace, harmony, and reconciliation wherever you go."

Then Dr. Marney pointed his finger at the student, "But if you allow life to sour you, anger, jealousy, and resentment will be your constant companions. They will lie with you in your grave."

"Experiencing Forgiveness For Ourselves"

George Ballanchine choreographed a ballet of the story of the prodigal son as recorded in the Bible. There is a very moving scene depicting the return of the son to the father. The father is seen at the far side of the stage, standing with his arms folded in front of him. The son enters on his knees on the opposite side of the stage. Painfully, the prodigal son pulls himself across the stage toward his father, his arms outstretched, and his face pleading for forgiveness. The father remains immobile. He stands staring sternly down at the son. With excruciating agony, the son crawls to his father's feet. He begins to pull himself up on the father's robes. All the time he is begging to be received back into the father's love, the father looks sternly, arms crossed in front of him. Then, as the music builds to a great crescendo the father finally opens his arms to receive the son.

It is a very moving ballet. It is choreographed well. It is hard to watch it with dry eyes. However, it is not the story of the prodigal son as told by Jesus. In the story of the prodigal son recorded in the Bible, the father goes out each day and looks down the road to see if his son has returned. In the story told by Jesus, when the father sees the son coming he does not stand immobile. No, he runs down the road to meet his son. With his arms wide open he shouts, "Welcome home! Welcome home! That which was lost is now found. That which was dead has been made alive. Welcome home! Welcome home!"

Into all of our lives disappointment, betrayal, and defeat will come. We have a choice. We can allow these hurts to harden our hearts or we can use them to develop forgiving hearts. We can grow bitter or we can grow in grace. When we come to terms with the things that we have done and the things that we have left undone in this life, do we dare choose not to be forgiving? When we consider all that the Heavenly Father has forgiven us, who can presume to do less for those who ask our forgiveness? A forgiving heart is a heart that has experienced forgiveness for itself.

If you know something about failure and defeat...

If you know what it is to do those things you thought you would never do...

If you know what it is to leave undone those things you thought it would be unthinkable not to do...

If you have suffered pain for the sins that you have caused others...

Then you know something about the love, mercy, and grace of God, because it is alive within you.

You know about forgiveness because you have experienced it for yourself. A forgiving heart is a heart that has experienced forgiveness for itself. A forgiving heart grows out of self-examination. A judgmental, resentful heart is the product of focusing on the deficiencies in others while ignoring ones own. The forgiving heart has experienced forgiveness for itself. We have stated repeatedly in this book that forgiving is not easy. However, when we take an honest look at ourselves, forgiving those who have hurt us does become a lot easier.

When all is said and done, we will be given plenty of opportunities in our life journey to forgive those who have hurt us. We will be given plenty of opportunity to stand in need of grace from others. There are many gifts that we can give ourselves in this life. One of the greatest gifts that we can give ourselves is to nurture a forgiving heart. With a forgiving heart we are in a better position to get our lives back when another attempts to take them from us. **Forgive and get your life back can become a reality that brings healing and wholeness.**

QUESTIONS FOR REFLECTION AND/OR ACTION

1. How would you explain to another person your understanding that the power to forgive is one of God's miracles?

2. How do you think God could take your hurt and pain and use it to transform you into a more loving, compassionate, forgiving person?

3. Have you had previous experiences in your life when God took garbage and turned it into gold? When? What? How?

4. How would you explain to another person that a forgiving heart is a heart that has experienced forgiveness for itself?

Summary

"You Look Hurt"

We can remain anchored to the past. We can remain the prisoners of those who have hurt us. We can go to our graves demanding justice. Or we can choose not to let them hold us hostage. We can choose to forgive. When we make that choice, we set ourselves free. We release ourselves from their control. We get our lives back.

It was three decades ago that I saw the movie. It was being shown on a religious retreat. It made an incredible impact on me. It was about a young man by the name of Jim Hendrix. Jim was driving home after having a couple of drinks with some friends. He was cruising along a residential boulevard in his car. Then from out of nowhere a young girl about twelve years of age stepped in front of his car. He put on his brakes, but his car hit the little girl. She was taken to the hospital.

Over the next few weeks, the police clears Jim and the insurance company clears him. His constant litany is, "It was not my fault." Still, he was restless. He was touchy. He could not sleep at night. His friends suggested that perhaps he should go see the little girl. To this, he would reply, "It was not my fault."

Sleep deprived, he finally made an appointment with a psychiatrist who was also a friend. He wanted some sleeping pills. The psychiatrist said to him, "Friend to friend, I don't think you need sleeping pills. I think you need to go see the little girl."

Jim became angry. "I told you that it was not my fault. The police told me it was not my fault."

To this the psychiatrist replied, "Well, then, legally you should be able to sleep."

Finally, Jim relented, and went to the hospital to visit the little girl. When he walked into the room, he could see that the little girl was in a body cast. He walked up to the side of the bed and looked down on her. The little girl saw him and said, "You're Mister Hendrix, aren't you?"

"Yes," he replied with a shaking voice. "How did you know it was me?"

Her response was classic, "You look hurt."

He then apologized to the little girl and asked if she would forgive him. The little girl's response to his tearful plea was, "I already have."

Whether you are the person who has been betrayed or you are the betrayer, the end result is pain and suffering for both. Unless the betrayer is totally without any superego development, they will have lived in fear of having their secret discovered. Once their darkness is brought to light their pain and anxiety will increase in proportion to their acceptance of the pain they have caused. Only the most evil will fail to have any empathy for the person they have hurt.

For the betrayer, there will be consequences associated with their actions. They risk the loss of friends, or job, or love, or marriage, and for some, legal consequences. The ultimate goal for both the betrayer and the betrayed is to move from suffering to healing. Both must move beyond the event to regain their lives and their futures. As we have continually stated, forgiving is a process. Not every person will be able to move all the way through the process from forgiving to restoration. Some will not be able to complete all three stages in the forgiveness process. Still, healing can be found when we forgive, even if there is not reconciliation or restoration with those who have injured us.

What follows is a brief summary of the Forgiveness Process. My hope is that it can serve as a ready guide to move you through the process of forgiving. My prayer is that it will help you move from pain to healing.

The steps in the forgiving process may not be clearly delineated and may overlap. The important thing is to move intentionally through each step in the process.

STEP ONE
"CHOOSE TO FORGIVE"

When we slam our fingers in a car door, the pain will cause us to stop all other activity and focus on our injury. The world, for us, will cease to spin until we have gotten the pain under control. In the same way, when our heart is slammed by another person's deceit, lies, and betrayal, the pain will paralyze us. We need to walk into that pain. If we try to pretend that the betrayal did not happen, we only open ourselves to having the pain express itself in other ways. Many psycho-physical illnesses may be traced to underlying emotional hurt that has not been acknowledged. When we have been hurt we have a choice. We can look the other way and pretend that we have not been hurt. We can become a martyr, or we can choose to forgive.

TRUSTING PEOPLE ARE HAPPIER, MORE CONTENTED PEOPLE.

Obviously, when we slam our finger in the door, we will blame ourselves. "How could I have been so stupid? I should have known better." When someone betrays us, the temptation will be overwhelming to blame ourselves for being so trusting. The betrayal of trust is not information about us. It is information about the person who deceived us.

Studies show that people who have a high trust level are more trustworthy themselves. Trusting people are happier, more contented people. However, every person who is betrayed will invariably play "if only" as a part of the acceptance process. "If only I had taken more notice, been more careful, done things differently." All of these thoughts are to be expected. We must also constantly remind ourselves that we did not force the person to deceive us. They are responsible for their choice of sin. We are not.

Moving through this stage of the forgiving process is critical.

Even if those who have hurt us do not ask for our forgiveness, we must make a conscious decision to forgive them. When we make that decision, we are making the decision to move beyond the hurt and the pain. We are making the decision to not let another person's sin against us freeze our lives in a past trauma. We are making the decision to experience healing. We are making the decision to take our life back. We are making the decision to have a life beyond the past. We are making a decision to claim the promise of the future. Carpe Diem, "Seize the Day," becomes our motto.

Step Two
"Don't Cry Alone"

You have been hurt. You need an empathetic ear. You need some consoling words. Talk to a trusted clergy person. Bring them into your confidence. Let them know the pain that you are carrying. Ask them to pray with you and to give you spiritual direction. You need them to help you make sure that you are moving through the forgiving process. You must guard against turning the anger in on yourself and becoming depressed. You may also need the support of others who have also experienced similar pain. Support groups for those who have been verbally and physically abused are abundant, as are support groups for others who have been victimized in so many different ways.

Step Three
"Do Get Angry"

If I step on your foot, you will tell me that it hurts. When another person steps on our hearts, we need to let them know it. The anger phase in the forgiving process is a time for "I statements." "I feel, I want, I need" all must be verbalized. Do not swallow your anger. Do not resort to "you statements." Do not give in to thoughts of revenge or getting even. Do not follow the axiom, "I don't get angry, I get even." Forget about getting even; get angry! Remind yourself, "Vengeance is mine says the Lord. I will repay."*

---

* Hebrews 10:30

The person who has hurt you needs to see your anger, if that is at all possible. They need to see that they have hurt you and you need to have the opportunity to verbally express your anger to them. Whether in writing or in person, you need to discharge your anger.

This is also a time to increase your physical activity. Get more exercise. Walk, run, lift weights, watch your diet, and take care of your body. Anger that is not discharged can take its toll on your health. Physical activity can be a great aid in discharging the anger.

STEP FOUR
"BURY THE PAST, TAIL AND ALL"

We will never be able to erase the trauma completely from our memory. We simply are not wired that way. We are wired to learn from the past. However, we can leave the past in the past. This is the essence of what it means to forgive and forget. When the memories of the past rear their head, we are resolved not to resuscitate them, but to put them back in the past where they belong. And absolutely, under no circumstances, do we throw the sins of the past in the face of the person we have forgiven. This last step in this stage of the forgiving process is the ribbon on the package. It is an essential step in our own healing.

STEP FIVE
"CHOOSE TO RECONCILE"

Before reconciliation is an option, the person that has sinned against us has to come to terms with the extent of the injury they have imposed. This means they take full responsibility for their action. No excuses. No blame. No justification. No rationalizations. Likewise, our pain must become their pain. Contrition is empathy in action. Contrition is feeling the hurt of the injured. Contrition is being so sorry for what we have done that if it were possible we would take all the pain of the person we have hurt upon ourselves.

When I was in grade school, I had a friend who enjoyed pulling practical jokes on me. Most were designed to embarrass and humiliate me in front of my fellow students. After every one had a good laugh at my expense, my friend was contrite. He would say, "I'm sorry. Friends?" I forgave him more times than common sense would dictate. Each time I forgave him; he would simply set me up again and then repeat the process. Perhaps I am a slow learner, but after awhile, I realized his contrition was not real and his friendship was certainly not needed.

Before reconciling with a person who has injured us, we need to satisfy ourselves that they are truly sorry for the pain that they have caused us. They are not just being sorry because they got caught, to avoid the consequences of their actions, or to get back into our good graces so they can hurt us again. I fear that this is a process of spiritual discernment. We will need to trust our instincts, our intuition, and our gut reactions. It will be a time for much prayer.

Before reconciling with them, we need to satisfy ourselves that they will make the necessary amendments in their behavior to assure us that they will not hurt us again in quite the same way. If they have stolen from us, will they make restitution? If they have been unfaithful to us, will they cease communication with the person they betrayed us with? Will they go to therapy to gain help for their insecurities that led them to the betrayal? Will they seek spiritual direction to help them fight their temptations? What amendments are they willing to make? What evidence can they present that life with them will be different if we reconcile with them?

This is a critical stage in the reconciliation process. Do not move through it casually or too quickly.

There is an old expression, "Sleep with one eye open." You do not want to spend the rest of your life living in fear that the person is going to hurt you again. Just as talking about your hurt and pain with them is an essential part of phase one; it is equally critical that you talk about your future together. How is it going to be different? What are your respective expectations? What will be your common goals? How will you communicate your needs and disappointments to one another? What can you do together to insure that the past does not repeat itself? Old habits must disappear. New habits must be developed in their place.

To make the reconciliation complete, you will need to keep the channels of communication open. You will need to have scheduled check-ups with a spiritual director, therapist, or other professional guide. The purpose of the checkups with a third party is to give you the opportunity to further redefine your relationship as needed. The business world uses management consultants for this purpose. Friends, life partners, and families need relationship consultants. In time, the reconciliation will not only bring further healing, but also a new positive energy will replace the old habits.

STEP SIX
"RESTORATION"

Restoration means that we are going to completely bring the person back into our lives without reservation or condition. In fact, restoration is unconditional love in action. We can reconcile with a life partner who has betrayed us, but that does not necessarily mean that we will restore them to our marriage bed. In fact, it may mean just the opposite. We may divorce them, but continue to wish the very best for them at all times. At the very heart of loving our enemies is rising above the desire to get excited at their downfall. To love our enemies is to wish them well in all things. We can reconcile with an employee who has stolen from us, but that does not mean we are going to give them the combination to the office safe.

> **TO LOVE OUR ENEMIES IS TO WISH THEM
> WELL IN ALL THINGS.**

Restoration, on the other hand, means that the person assumes their former position in our life with complete and total trust. It is restoring an unfaithful spouse to the marriage bed. It is giving an employee that has stolen from us the combination to the safe. Restoration is the most difficult part of the forgiving process. To borrow the words of the marriage service in the Book of Common Prayer, "It must not be done lightly or unadvisedly, but reverently, deliberately."*

The Father of the Prodigal Son in the parable told by Jesus did not have a professional to call upon. Such is life in a parable. In real life, however, restoration should not be attempted without professional guidance. An ongoing relationship with a spiritual director will be needed to make sure that the marital relationship stays on track. I am certain that there are couples that can bring healing to a broken relationship through their own efforts. I can't help but imagine all self-effort as being very tiring. God provides a source of healing that will delightfully surprise those who put the Almighty at the center of their efforts.

The same is true for a business relationship. Spiritual guidance is an absolute must. Restoration can only succeed in

* Book of Common Prayer, page 423

the context of prayer and spiritual support. Friends, business associates, partners in life will be nurtured by being a part of a worshiping community and regularly worshiping together. The truth in the old axiom, "Couples who pray together, stay together" will be discovered fully in this phase of restoration.

There are many religious ceremonies that can be adapted to celebrate the return of the Prodigal. Couples may want to have their homes blessed or renew their marriage vows. Families may want to welcome back a rebellious child with a family service of commitment. Business partners may want to adapt a new logo and have their offices blessed. The possibilities are manifold. The most important part is that there is a time of prayer, and blessing, and commitment to a new life together. It is a time for celebration. "Bring a robe, a ring, and a fatted calf. That which was lost has been found. That which was dead has been made alive again."*

If you end the forgiving process without reconciling with the person who hurt you, you will still have given yourself a great gift. You will have moved from hurt to healing. If reconciliation is an option for you, I pray that you will "Seize the Day." Likewise, restoration may not be an option, and in some circumstances, it may not even be advisable. If, however, restoration is an alternative, it can be an occasion for a great feast.

STEP SEVEN
"NURTURE A
FORGIVING HEART"

From the beginning I have tried to emphasize that forgiving is a spiritual process. It may be some of the hardest work we ever do. You can do it! No, you must do it! For your own

---

* Luke 15:22-24

health and happiness, you must do it! You, however, will not have to do it alone. God will give you the grace and strength to do what must be done. The prayers of the people of every faith will sustain you. I will add my prayers to theirs. It will be a mighty force of positive energy, encompassing both heaven and earth. This supernatural power can see you through even though you might grow weary on occasion. Forgiving is a spiritual process.

It is my earnest prayer that you will not attempt the forgiveness process without calling on God or your Higher Power as you know them. The world is full of people who are literally "bent over" from trying to carry their burdens all alone. We do not have to walk stooped over with the hurt and the pain of the world riding on our shoulders. We do not have to let our own hurt bend our backs and cripple our posture. We can walk through life standing upright. We can smile and look others in the eye, even those who have hurt us. We can be set free of the burden and hurt that weighs us down. We need only forgive those who have injured us. Often, we need to seek forgiveness for ourselves and forgive ourselves. It is a spiritual process. You can do it. You will be thankful that you have done so.

FORGIVE, AND GET YOUR LIFE BACK!

THE PROMISE

The story is told of a little girl in a remote village who reported to her parents that she was having conversations with God. Her faith was so sincere and her descriptions so believable that the parents reported her experiences to the village priest. The priest was also astounded by what appeared to be a truly miraculous event. The priest reported the happenings to the bishop.

The bishop came to the village church for a visitation. He interviewed the little girl. He decided to test her experience. "Next time you talk to God," the bishop counseled her, "Ask God to list for you the sins that this bishop reported in his last confession."

A few weeks went by and the bishop returned to the village to meet with the little girl. "Did you ask God to list for you the sins that this bishop recited in his last confession?"

"Yes, I asked God for a list of your sins," the little girl responded.

"And what did God tell you?" the bishop asked.

The little girl began to laugh and dance around the room. "God told me that He forgot!"

A FORGIVENESS PRAYER

Practice the following prayer on a daily basis. Insert the name(s) of the person(s) you need to forgive in the blank spaces.

"Dear God, I am so tired of hurting. I don't want to live my life feeling angry. I don't like the empty feeling in my heart. I am weary of having my stomach tied in knots. I don't want to feel bitter. Holy One, give me the grace to forgive _____. Remove the anger that I feel for _____ from my heart. Clothe me with compassion for _____ and the blindness that allowed them to hurt me.

_____, you are now forgiven. I forgive you for hurting me. God has put away your sin against me.

And now through the power of the Spirit I claim the healing of memories God has promised me. Through that same power I now release the hurt and the pain. Thank you, God for setting me free. Thank you for giving me my life back. Thank you for showing me how to laugh, love, and live again.

I ask this through Jesus Christ who forgave and healed all those who came to him for help. Amen."